I0568053

Miracles in the Midst of Storms

60 years of God's Faithfulness

Ann R. Wilson

A Certain Woman

Miracles in the Midst of Storms
60 years of God's Faithfulness
Ann R.Wilson
A Certain Woman

Miracles in the Midst of Storms
Copyright © 2014 Ann Wilson
Copyright © 2022 Reprint With Part 2
Second Edition
ISBN: 978-1-955759-22-9

Cover Design by Sarah Haynes
For information on how to receive a copy, please contact Ann's
daughter, Lynn Passfield at (928) 499-8857

All Scripture quotations are from:
Scripture quotations marked "KJV" are taken from the Holy Bible,
King James Version (Public Domain).
Scripture taken from the New King James Version®. copyright © 1982
by Thomas Nelson. Used by permission. All rights reserved.
Scripture quotations marked (NIV) are taken from the Holy Bible, New
International Version®, NIV®.
Copyright © 1973, 1978, 1984 by Biblica, Inc.™
Used by permission of Zondervan. All rights reserved worldwide.
http://www.zondervan.com
Scripture quotations marked (NLT) are taken from the Holy Bible, New
Living Translation, copyright ©1996, 2004, 2015 by Tyndale House
Foundation. Used by permission of Tyndale House Publishers, Carol
Stream, Illinois 60188. All rights reserved.

TABLE OF CONTENTS

ii

iv

ADDENDUM
Part 2

FOREWORD
By Russ Womack

Author Ann Wilson writes with boldness and honesty as she invites all readers to walk with her through 60 years of her personal storms, and God's miracles that sustained and strengthened her through it all. This autobiography encourages us to both recognize and be cognizant of the frequently overlooked miracles in life that requires, among other things, a confident humility. Ann's complete confidence in the power, love, and grace of Jesus Christ produces depth to the pages, while her humility dictates that without God's authority and direction, her life is empty and meaningless. The words breathe a safe, maternal truth where childlike innocence fosters effortless acceptance in miracles. She chooses to illuminate her autobiography in the protective shadow of Christ, honest and personal, a courageous transparency that can accurately discern such contemplations as "Every answer to prayer is a miracle."

After reading "Miracles in the Midst of Storms," I can say with absolute assurance that this is a must read for all audiences. If you don't believe in miracles at the turn of page one, or believe at a safe distance, I'm convinced that you will relax into a state where possibilities reign louder than doubt, and perhaps even hold tight to the belief that you also receive miracles – miracles that are offered with outstretched hands straight from the love and grace of God. The words contained within these pages remind us that miracles aren't only a thing of the past, lifted from the dirt roads of Galilee, but rather a very real and tangible yesterday, today, and tomorrow, sketched upon streets with names such as Hurt, Lost, Hopelessness, Despair.

Miracles in the Midst of Storms is effectively divided into three chronological sections: the early, middle, and later years. The early years depict a young Ann Wilson as she searches for meaning through the first round of storms in her life, and the necessity of submitting to Christ to take over her life and to lead her through life's corridors. By the time the middle years approach, you'll find yourself no longer nameless in the audience, but rather sitting one on one with Ann. With each turn of a page, an easy familiarity pushes through. You'll soon realize that her miracles are no more frequent nor greater than yours. There's a sense of camaraderie between author and reader alongside a nudge of the soul that says every answered prayer might just be a miracle. Before long, you are invited to the later years.

It takes time to build trust, time to build faith, time to recognize with confident humility that miracles are being placed in your hands every day. By now you are, in a sense, part of her family, a casual listener, effortlessly seeing your own miracles breaking through the veils of your storms. Don't be apologetic if you find yourself drifting off while reading, remembering aged miracles while scanning through these pages. That's right where Ann wants you to be, because when you have conviction of your own personal miracles, you won't ever again miss recognizing the One who personally and eagerly hands them to you.

ACKNOWLEDGMENTS

I first want to thank Randy Vanesian, Pastor of Living Faith Church for his inspirational messages that inspired me to write this book. It was his message one Sunday morning entitled "Remembering the Miracles," and his challenge to the congregation to list the miracles of our past. They are the things that give us hope and faith for the future. As I began to jot down just a few things, I realized there was a lot more than I had first imagined.

I want to thank Rebecca Riviere for editing, helping me with my first manuscript giving me encouraging words; also Russell Womack who edited the second draft, prodding me onward when I was almost ready to quit. Thank you also, Angie Tessitore, for your words of wisdom and encouragement.

My children and my husband helped strengthen my resolve to finish. My daughter, Lynn, helped immensely, finding photos and other finishing touches, especially dates and years.

There were times when I felt this was "senseless" and wanted to quit, but many of my friends and family members pushed me forward with words of encouragement to bring it to completion. Thanks to you all!

INTRODUCTION

The reason this book is written is to remember God's faithfulness and His miracles, affecting me, my children, my extended family and friends.

There is no difficulty in this life that God can't help us get through when we trust Him. There is no one else to go to in times of trouble, except God, and there is no stopping place – we must keep pressing on. *"...but he that endureth to the end shall be saved."* (Matthew 10:22b) Sometimes we can't see the results of our prayers immediately, but God is always working. While we're going through the storm, it may look like we're going to fail, that we just can't make it, *"but with God all things are possible."* (Matthew 19:26b). I have been through many storms, even when I thought there was absolutely no way out – I was sunk – yet here I am at 79 years old still trusting Him, and fighting the battle because of God's faithfulness. I've made it through many storms over the years, and am still pressing on. My hope is in Him. He is my life and my strength. He has begun a good work in me, and He will complete it. *"Being confident of this very thing, that he which hath begun a good work in you will perform it until the day of Jesus Christ:"* (Philippians 1:6)

He answers prayer in ways we may never dream possible. His answer is always better than we could have imagined. Yes, He is the miracle worker!

God is no respecter of persons. You don't realize when and how you're changing, but our journeys are one step at a time, a little here, a little there. After sixty years, I realize how much I've changed and how faithful God has been in leading me.

In this book I hope to show how God has led me through my storms and hope to encourage you to trust Him. God will not fail you. He will complete the work He has begun in you.

As I set out to write this journal of my remembrances and the miracles God has done in my life, I realize that every answer to prayer is a miracle. There were so many that I didn't know where to begin. I decided that my first personal encounter with Jesus, and the salvation of my soul, was my first miracle. And so, here my story begins....

Chapter 1

THE EARLY YEARS

Ann - High School Graduation Day - May, 1953

GOD – ARE YOU REALLY UP THERE?

❧

"And it shall come to pass that whoever calls on the name of the Lord shall be saved."
Acts 2:21 NKJV

The year was 1953; I was still 17 years old, and it was about a month before my 18th birthday. I had graduated from High School the previous May, left home, went to California, and tried making it on my own. Finally, just a few months later, after nearly starving to death, I called my father to ask for help. He sent me money to come home, and never said a word about my decisions.

The next morning, as I sat alone at the kitchen table, after my sister and brother had gone off to school, and my Dad had gone to work, I looked up and said "God, are you really up there?" I continued with something like "God, I'm 17 years old and my life has been a total waste so far. I need to know what's real. Are you really real? Is everything I've been taught in Sunday School and Church really true? Do you really care about me? Can you hear me? Somehow, God, (if you're really up there) show me beyond a shadow of doubt that you really exist. I have to know!" Then I said "God, if you're really real and you're hearing my prayer, cause me to get a job tomorrow, and go to work at the first place I walk in to." I thought this would be a pretty hard challenge for anyone, even God.

As far back as I could remember I had always gone to Church and Sunday school. At the age of 10, I publicly confessed Jesus as my Lord and Savior and was baptized in a Baptist Church. I wanted to be a good person, acceptable to God and man. I tried to obey my father, please my teachers, treat people fairly according to the rules of the church and the Ten Commandments, but now I felt empty and lost; I didn't know where to go or whom to turn to. I never had a mother to turn to for advice or help, and my father didn't know how to talk to me. I never really had a personal relationship with Jesus, even though I was baptized earlier. I didn't understand the full meaning of baptism, nor what salvation was really all about. Now I felt I had to know "everything!" After I prayed that morning, I suddenly felt a great peace come over me; I knew my prayer was going to be answered. I knew God was real and that I was going to find a job the next day.

The next morning, I got up early and asked Dad if I could get a ride into town with him. He said, "okay," but seemed a little puzzled about where I was going. When he asked me, I told him I was going to work. He asked me where, and I said I didn't know yet, but I would catch a bus home at the end of the day. He never questioned me about that any further and was silent the rest of the trip. He dropped me off in downtown Phoenix, on Washington Street, where most of the department and "five and dime" stores were. I went into Newberry's, found my way to the upstairs office, walked in boldly and said that I would like to go to work for them. Did they have an opening?

It just happened that the floor manager was there with the bookkeeper and had just fired a girl. She asked if I

4

could go to work immediately. I said that I could, and she said "follow me." From that day on, I never doubted the existence of God. I had great peace that all was well with my soul. I didn't know where I was going from there, but I knew everything was okay.

That was my first "personal" encounter with Jesus. When He came into my heart, He gave me faith to believe in Him, and trust Him. I would like to say that I never had any problems after that, but I had a lot of problems, trials and tests. I had lots to learn about "walking" with Him. I was like a newborn baby, full of faith and trust, yet had *so much to learn!*

REFLECTION

It's not difficult to be saved. He bore all our sins upon His own body on the cross. We just have to believe and accept his substitutionary sacrifice by faith and confess Him as our Lord and Savior. The thief on the cross who was crucified with Jesus, changed his destiny and eternal future by simply saying to Jesus, *"Lord, remember me when You come into Your kingdom."* He expressed his belief in Jesus by the words he spoke, and was asking for help. Jesus heard his heart's cry and replied *"Today you will be with Me in Paradise."* (Luke 23:43 NKJV)

Jesus loves us so much and gives us every opportunity to come to Him. He is longsuffering and patient with us. It is His will that all should come to repentance and be saved. *"He is not willing that any should perish..."* (2 Peter 3:9b)

That if you confess with your mouth the Lord Jesus and believe in your heart that God has raised Him from the dead, you will be saved. For with the heart one believes unto righteous-

5

ness, and with the mouth confession is made unto salvation. (Romans 10:9-10 NKJV)

For God so loved the world that He gave His only begotten Son, that whoever believes in Him should not perish but have everlasting life. (John 3:16-17 NKJV)

We don't have to pray a long prayer, or beg, or do some special work. We just have to cry out "Lord, help me!" Scripture also tells us that we are a new creation, when the Spirit of God comes to dwell within us.

After I prayed that day at the kitchen table, I felt clean and whole, like a great weight was lifted off my shoulders, and I knew everything in my life was okay. I truly believed in my heart that God was real, Jesus was my Lord, and He had heard and answered my prayer. I was a brand new person.

"Therefore, if anyone is in Christ, he is a new creation; old things have passed away; behold, all things have become new." (2 Corinthians 5:17 NKJV)

MOVING FORWARD

But as it is written: "Eye has not seen, nor ear heard, nor have entered into the heart of man the things which God has prepared for those who love Him."
1 Corinthians 2:9 NKJV

Soon after my conversion, I met Bill Passfield. I was introduced to him by a friend, and after a two week courtship, we were married in Phoenix, at my Pastor's home.

Bill was a long way from his home in Idaho, and wanted to get married. I wanted to get out of my father's house, so we were a perfect couple. He was a sailor stationed at Litchfield Park, so we lived near the base. This was a long way from my church home in Phoenix, that I had known since I was 12. I didn't know where else to go to church in our new community, so I just didn't go anywhere.

I became busy adjusting to my new life, and starting a family. Billy was my first child, and was born at the base hospital in Litchfield Park. When Bill had to "ship out" to Korea, we moved to Ventura, California, where his parents lived. I was pregnant with my second child (Kathy). I stayed there until he returned home.

7

Ann & Bill - 1953

Billy, 2 mos.

Kathy - 4 mos

Ann with Billy, 1 yr. & Kathy 1 wk.

Kathy was born at the Port Hueneme Naval base hospital, a couple of months before he came home. When Bill returned home, we moved to Glendale, Oregon, where he had an uncle who had promised he could help Bill find some work. Little did I know my life was going to change radically and forever.

Even though I had been out of church since I got married, and had not thought much about God for a while, God had not forgotten me. I learned that He doesn't let us go so easily. He has ways of drawing us back to Him (or, at least, getting our attention).

It was while we were living in Glendale, Oregon, that a young, minister friend from the church I had attended in Phoenix, found out from the senior pastor where I was living. He wrote to me, and said he was going through the area and would like to stop by and see me. By this time, I had started to try to find a church home. There were only three churches in the vicinity.

Since I was from a Reformed Presbyterian Church in Phoenix, I decided to try the Presbyterian Church first. It was a bad experience, since I spent the entire time in the nursery with my two babies, Billy and Kathy; I could do that at home. Then I tried the Baptist church at one of their evening services and left the children home with Bill. It didn't seem to be what I was looking for either. No one greeted me, or even noticed I was there. Since the only other church in the area was an Assembly of God, and I had heard that they were Pentecostal, I was a little apprehensive about going there. My father had always told me they were of the devil. He said that I should never go near them; therefore I didn't know what to do.

When this minister friend came to visit, he asked me if I had been going to church anywhere. I explained the circumstances to him about the Presbyterian and Baptist church, and then said, "The only one left is an Assembly of God church, and I sure can't go there," expecting he

9

would understand. Then he surprised me by saying "I have a couple of good friends that I met in college, and they are Assembly of God members. They are very good people, I highly respect them." I was a little puzzled and curious, especially when he said, "I think you ought to give it a try." To this day, I think God must have inspired him to come visit us. I hadn't really known him that well, and it had been a long time since I left Phoenix, but, because of his recommendation, I decided to give the Assembly of God Church a try.

I first went to an evening service and was warmly received. When I entered the church, immediately several young people came over to me. A couple of them gave me a hug and said how glad they were to see me; they were so warm and kind toward me, I thought they must have mistaken me for someone else. I had never been in a church where people were so friendly. One girl said, "Come on over and sit with me." I felt like I had known these people forever. They showed so much kindness and love toward me that it made me a little uncomfortable. As a child I had never experienced or heard much about love. I had a hard time knowing how to respond to these people. This church was not like any other that I had attended before; people raised their hands when they sang, and went to the altar to pray. In growing up, I believe I might have thought obedience and love were the same thing. I had never experienced anyone ever hugging me or telling me they loved me, or treating me with such kindness. This new experience was strange and I was enjoying it cautiously and suspiciously, at first.

One evening I saw the strangest, most wonderful thing that I had ever seen in my life. I was sitting on the front row and this girl was praying at the altar. Her face shone so bright, that when she looked up with her hands raised, I thought she must be talking directly to God, but in a most strange language. About that time, the pastor's wife must have seen the curious look on my face; she sat down beside me and asked if I knew what was happening, I said, "no, but it sure looks wonderful."

She turned in her Bible to Acts 2:1-4 and read to me about the disciples being filled with the Holy Spirit on the day of Pentecost, then she read Acts 2:38 & 39 "...

Repent, and let every one of you be baptized in the name of Jesus Christ for the remission of sins; and you shall receive the gift of the Holy Spirit. For the promise is to you and to your children, and to all who are afar off, as many as the Lord our God will call." (NKJV)

When she read verse 39 and the part about the promise being to all that are afar off, I knew that it meant me also. I was overwhelmed and excited about this new information. *THIS MEANT ME!* My heart was stirred with hunger for this great experience.

In all the years I had attended church, I never read those particular scriptures or heard them preached. It was hard to believe that people could be so blessed while on this earth. I thought you had to die and go to heaven before you could obtain such joy. I wanted to know more about all of this, as soon as possible. Someone told me to begin reading my Bible, and read it as though it is God's "love letter" especially to me. I began to read my Bible every spare minute. Every day, as soon as my housework was finished, I would read the Bible. I couldn't get enough. I had fallen in love with the Word. It became my life, and the most treasured thing I had ever known. It became my roadmap of how to live and please God.

Bill became angry every time he came home and caught me reading. He said I had become a fanatic and he was very verbal about disliking the changes he saw in me. We began to have problems with our marriage and I wasn't wise in knowing how to handle things. I tried to put my Bible away quickly when I saw him coming home. I would read only while he was gone, but it didn't help.

I was so hungry spiritually, that I went to a two week teaching seminar called "The Spirit Himself." It met every night. Bill didn't want to go with me, so he watched the kids. He never complained, but wasn't interested, so I went alone.

REFLECTION

God alone knows the heart of every individual. He knew just where to take me to hear the words I needed to hear to build my faith to attain everlasting life with Him.

If you're hungry for God, He will take you to the ends of the earth if necessary, or send someone to you, that you might hear the things you need to hear to draw you close to Him, and give you eternal life.

I am still amazed today of the "wondrous salvation" that He has provided mankind, along with all the benefits and help to keep us in all our ways through life's journey.

> *"How shall we escape if we neglect <u>so great a salvation</u>, [emphasis added] which at the first began to be spoken by the Lord, and was confirmed to us by those who heard Him."* (Hebrews 2:3 NKJV)

I still thank God regularly for His *"<u>so great a salvation</u>."* His love for all of us is greater than we can ever comprehend; He is 100 percent "love." When I say "I love Him with all my heart," I realize it's only within the earthly capacity that I know of, but it's still important, and it's important for Him too.

DIVINE HEALING

"Is anyone among you sick? Let him call for the elders of the church, and let them pray over him, anointing him with oil in the name of the Lord. And the prayer of faith will save the sick, and the Lord will raise him up. And if he has committed sins, he will be forgiven."
James 5:14-15 - NKJV

I was so hungry for more of the Word of God – I couldn't learn fast enough. A whole new world had opened up to me. Every day was exciting with great expectation of what God was doing, and going to do, in my life. I didn't know what divine healing meant, but had heard some discussion about it. I was not a sickly person, and didn't really know what people were talking about.

One night when I came in to the service, the woman sitting next to me asked me if I felt alright. I told her I had a terrible headache that had lingered for nearly three weeks, and I couldn't get rid of it. It made me very sick at times, but I always went on doing what I was doing without taking medication. It was just the way my Dad had raised us, and to me it was normal to put up with discomfort. He always said "It'll go away," or "It'll be alright." Usually it did.

The woman I was talking to, stood up in the service, and asked if they would pray for me, that I had a very bad headache. I was petrified, embarrassed, and wanted to run out of the church; however, I didn't want to make this any bigger, so when they asked me to come up for prayer, I calmly and quietly walked up. The pastor and his wife, very calmly laid their hands on me, and said a prayer on my behalf. I just turned and hurried back to my seat, not knowing what to expect.

After a few minutes, I felt a little strange, and as I tried to analyze what the difference was, I realized that my headache was completely gone. This was my first miracle healing. I was discovering God in a whole new light and it was so very wonderful.

REFLECTION

It was not my faith that brought about my healing, since I had no idea what to expect. I also had not asked for prayer, but another asked for me. I also did not have any "unbelief," because I had not even heard of it before. God heals by either a person's own faith, or by the faith of another person, which is what happened in my case. The pastor and his wife prayed the prayer of agreement on my behalf.

"Again I say unto you, that if two of you shall agree on earth as touching any thing that they shall ask, it shall be done for them of my Father which is in heaven." (Matthew 18:19)

When someone is in need, and especially if they ask for prayer, this is our opportunity to join our faith with theirs in prayer. The prayer of agreement is one of the most common and effective ways to pray for a need.

Our healing is also part of the New Testament covenant promise as is mentioned in Isaiah and also by Peter in the following scripture:

> *"Who his own self bare our sins in his own body on the tree, that we, being dead to sins, should live unto righteousness: by whose stripes ye were healed."* (1 Peter 2:24 KJV)

CONVICTION OF SIN

"My little children, these things write I unto you, that ye sin not. And if any man sin, we have an advocate with the Father, Jesus Christ the righteous: and he is the propitiation for our sins: and not for ours only, but also for the sins of the whole world."
1 John 2:1-2 KJV

Once, while I was sitting in church, the pastor had asked if anyone in the congregation wanted to come forward for salvation and to accept Jesus as their Savior. I sat there thinking, "I don't need to go up there. I'm okay – this message is for someone else." Suddenly, I felt the presence of Jesus standing behind me. I could see Him even though He was above and behind my left shoulder. I was looking forward, but my Spirit must have turned and looked at Him, because I was looking right at Him even though he was behind me. He was looking at me and was very sad. He was not condemning, but sad, because He saw my sins. I felt guilty of the sin of lying. Lying is the devil's trademark, while Truth is God's hallmark. Jesus said, *He was the way, the truth and the life* (John 14:6). When I was 13 years old, I was reading the

Bible one day, and began to read Proverbs 12:22 *"Lying lips are abomination to the Lord: but they that deal truly are His delight."*

I thought to myself "Wow! I've lied a lot of times, and God really hates it. An 'abomination' sounds really bad." At that earlier time in my life, I worked on it some, but soon fell back into the old ways of the world.

I suddenly felt very sorry for my sins, and for making Jesus so sad. I began crying uncontrollably as I asked Him to forgive me, and help me to never lie or sin again. I had always thought of God as being very strict and judgmental when people sinned, ready to cut them off and send them to hell; now I saw Him in a whole new light. I didn't want Him to be sad over my sins, but I wanted His acceptance and love. I truly repented of everything I had ever done to make Him so unhappy.

REFLECTION

All people lie. Many lie frequently, without even realizing it. They think it is necessary to lie sometimes, to keep from hurting other's feelings, or others are better off not knowing the truth, or they just lie rather than speak the truth.

I have since learned that deception is another form of lying, as well as partial truths. God help us all to walk in truth according to Your Word.

"I have no greater joy than to hear that my children walk in truth." (3 John 4-5 KJV)

TONGUES OF FIRE

৩৯৫৩

"When the Day of Pentecost had fully come, they were all with one accord in one place. And suddenly there came a sound from heaven, as of a rushing mighty wind, and it filled the whole house where they were sitting. Then there appeared to them divided tongues, as of fire, and one sat upon each of them. And they were all filled with the Holy Spirit and began to speak with other tongues, as the Spirit gave them utterance."
Acts 2:1-4 NKJV

As the two week seminar at the church on "The Spirit Himself," began to come to a close, I knew I had to have the baptism of the Holy Spirit and the experience of tongues. People began to advise me of how to pray: One person told me to ask for diversity of tongues, *so I did*; another told me to ask for the gift of tongues and interpretation, *so I did*; another told me to just praise Jesus and *I did*; but nothing happened … *right away*. I told my mother-in-law that I didn't understand, because the Bible says to ask, and I did ask, and nothing happened. She told me I had to be more patient, and keep asking, *so I did.*

About three weeks after the classes on the Holy Spirit, when I was sitting in church one evening, God spoke to me about something I should give up. It was something personal that was important to me, and I believe it was a test to see if I loved it more than I loved Him. It was something I had just purchased that morning. I thought about it for just a fleeting second, but knew it was nothing in comparison to my new found life. I said, immediately, "Yes. Lord, I'll do it." I felt I had found a treasure that meant more to me than anything in this world, and nothing could even begin to compare to it. I wondered why more people didn't know about this Holy Spirit baptism. It was something greater than I could hardly fathom, that we could live in this world and be so blessed. I wanted Jesus and the baptism of the Holy Spirit more than anything else in the world. When I went to the altar that night, for the first time, while I was praying, my mouth and lips felt funny, sort of thick and numb. Everyone was beginning to leave the altar, so I thought I should too. I felt like something wonderful had just happened and I "knew" I was going to receive the baptism in the Holy Spirit very soon.

Due to some of the problems Bill and I had been having, he took some time off from work and went back to Arizona, to look for work there. I think he thought that if he could get us back to Arizona, near my Dad, he would be more comfortable leaving me.

This particular night, after I went home from church, a teenage neighbor girl that lived in the trailer park near us, wanted to spend the night, since Bill was gone to Arizona. Shortly after we went to bed, she fell sound asleep.

My mind was still on the wonderful worship service and what was happening in my spiritual life. I said to myself, "I can hardly wait for tomorrow night – I know I'm going to receive the baptism in the Holy Spirit." I was saying this over and over, eyes closed, and trying to go to sleep. Suddenly my arms began to rise while I was totally relaxed, and not of my own will. I began to feel the "anointing" on my lips and all through me. I decided to get up and go in the living room and pray.

I was just thanking and praising Jesus, for the wonderful blessings I had received and for what I knew He was going to do. I'm not sure how long I had been praying or sitting there, when I began to hear someone talking in a strange language that wasn't English. I suddenly realized that it was me talking, and that realization didn't even slow me down or startle me. It was like something natural that I had done all my life. I sat there for the longest time praying in tongues. I don't remember what time I finally went to bed, I just know that I had such a powerful anointing, that even the next day I could hardly talk to anyone. It was like my tongue was too thick, my lips and mouth were sort of numb and it was hard for me to form English words.

"Though I speak with the tongues of men and of angels, but have not love, I have become sounding brass or a clanging cymbal." (1 Corinthians 13:1 NKJV)

REFLECTION

I believe the gift of tongues is the language of angels. When we pray in tongues we have a direct line to God that Satan cannot intercept. When I am troubled about something and don't know exactly how to pray, I ask the Holy Spirit to pray through me by praying in tongues. The Holy Spirit always knows the will of God in any matter that concerns us.

Sometimes people pray in a known language of the world, that they themselves don't understand, but the hearer understands. This is what happened on the Day of Pentecost. It isn't always an angelic language, but I believe our prayer language is a language that only God understands.

We are also admonished to pray in the spirit and with the understanding as in the following scriptures:

"For if I pray in a tongue, my spirit prays, but my understanding is unfruitful. What is the conclusion then? I will pray with the spirit, and I will also pray with the understanding. I will sing with the spirit, and I will also sing with the understanding." (1 Corinthians 14:14-15 NKJV)

After the last supper when Judas had already left and Jesus knew his time was short he prepared and comforted his disciples, He let them know that even though they would not see him anymore, He would send them another comforter, the Holy Spirit, Who would be with them forever, and would be not only their comforter, but their teacher and would bring all things to their remembrance. When we receive the baptism in the Holy Spirit, all of this applies to us as well. Being filled with the Holy Spirit is not just about tongues, there is so much more. Jesus also said that we would receive power to witness for Him; we receive a special anointed boldness when the Holy Spirit comes upon us.

"And I will pray the Father, and he shall give you another Comforter, that he may abide with you forever; even the Spirit of truth; whom the world cannot receive, because it seeth him not, neither knoweth him: but ye know him; for He dwelleth with you, and shall be in you. I will not leave you comfortless: I will come to you." (John 14:16-18)

"But the Comforter, which is the Holy Ghost, whom the Father will send in my name, he shall teach you all things, and bring all things to your remembrance, whatsoever I have said unto you." (John 14: 26)

"Nevertheless I tell you the truth; It is expedient for you that I go away: for if I go not away, the Comforter will not come unto you; but if I depart, I will send him unto you." (John 16:7)

"But you shall receive power when the Holy Spirit has come upon you; and you shall be witnesses to Me in Jerusalem, and in all Judea and Samaria, and to the end of the earth." (Acts 1:8 NKJV)

I took all of these scriptures to myself as God's literal message to me. I learned to depend on the Holy Spirit as my personal counselor and guide. I talked to Him about everything in my life. When I look back over the years, I can see how the Holy Spirit taught me how to be a "real person," and how to live as an adult. He truly was my personal counselor, believe me, I needed one. It didn't make any difference how inconsequential the matter might have seemed to others, I would ask God about the matter. He already knew all about me, what was in my thoughts and mind, so it was easy to talk to Him about anything that I couldn't talk to others about.

I know the Holy Spirit guides and directs me into all truth, and many times when faced with a difficult problem, He would bring a scripture to my remembrance that I learned as a child. At that time in my life when I learned it, perhaps I didn't understand it, but when the Holy Spirit would bring it to my remembrance later, a greater understanding would come that applied to my current situation. If I had not learned that scripture, the Holy Spirit could not bring it to my remembrance. This is why it is so important that we study and learn the Word of God, and especially get it into our children's hearts and minds. It could be their salvation in the future.

MINISTERIAL SERVICE

"And God hath set some in the church, first apostles, secondarily prophets, thirdly teachers, after that miracles, then gifts of healings, helps, governments, diversities of tongues."
1 Corinthians 12:28 KJV

Soon after I was filled with the Holy Spirit I was asked to speak at the next Youth Meeting (ages 13-35). I was so anxious to serve and be a part of everything I could not say no to anything I was asked to do. Without realizing it, I was entering the "Ministry of Helps and Teaching."

I will never forget how nervous I was. For the first and only time in my life, when I was called on to come up and speak, I was actually so weak when I stood up that my knees were literally knocking. I had to stand for a few seconds before I could start walking up to the platform. To this day though, I remember the message I presented. I will never forget that day. Sometime later I was asked to become the Youth Leader, which I also accepted. They had a large group and I learned so much from everyone.

REFLECTION

If you want to be used of God, you must always make yourself available. It doesn't matter what you think you have been called to do, we have all been *called* to do good works.

"For we are his workmanship, created in Christ Jesus unto good works, which God hath before ordained that we should walk in them." (Ephesians 2:10)

You must be willing to do whatever you are asked, even if it is to clean the church. We have to learn to be obedient and faithful in the little things before God will use us in the greater things. God knows what He's preparing us for. Our part is to follow the leading of the Holy Spirit. He will open the doors as we are ready to go through them.

WATER BAPTISM
AND CONTINUING JOURNEY

❧

*"Then Peter said unto them, repent, and be
baptized every one of you in the name of Jesus
and ye shall receive the gift of the Holy Ghost."*
Acts 2:38 KJV

At the next baptismal service, I was baptized again in water, even though I had been baptized when I was younger, it was much more meaningful to me this second time. It doesn't hurt to be baptized more than once, especially if you feel you have come back to God with a deeper meaning and understanding of what salvation and water baptism is all about.

I continued going to services as often as possible. It was a good foundational church, and even though I was there less than a year, I was determined to go on with Jesus through eternity.

While in Oregon, we had lived in the same trailer park as Bill's parents who had moved there shortly after we did. His mother had been a Christian for many years, but didn't drive, so now she could go to church more

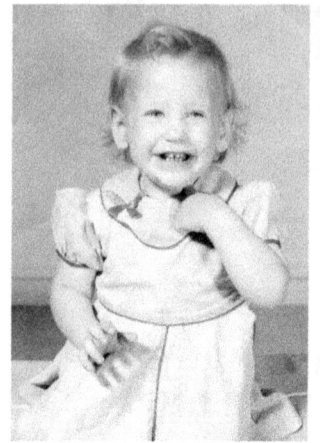

Kathy - 18 mos.

Ann holding Lynn, with
Kathy, Billy, and Bill - 1960

Left: Billy, Lynn,
& Kathy - 1960

Below: Lynn, 6 mos.

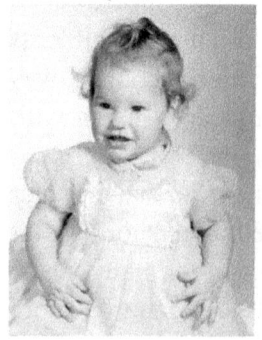

Ann - 1958

often with me. I went to church every time the doors were open. I couldn't get enough. It was a good time of bonding and she helped me a lot with spiritual things, and became my spiritual mentor. I still remember many of her words of advice. She was glad to get out more often and a great help to me.

I asked her once about the early church and all that the Christians went through, and how they were martyred. I said to her "I don't understand how anyone could go through the things that they did and remain true to God." I was especially overwhelmed about the story of Stephen. "I don't know if I could ever go through things like they did." Stephen even asked God to forgive those that were stoning him.

> *"And they stoned Stephen as he was calling on God and saying, 'Lord Jesus, receive my spirit.' Then he knelt down and cried out with a loud voice, 'Lord, do not charge them with this sin.' And when he had said this, he fell asleep."* (Acts 7:59-60 NKJV)

She told me very simply. Don't worry about things in the future. "You don't need dying grace until it's time to die. His grace is always sufficient to meet every need when you need it." I will never forget her answer. That can be applied to every area of our lives. *God's grace is sufficient.* (2 Corinthians 12:9)

I was changed, a *completely new* person when we finally moved back to California in 1958. By this time I was expecting my third child. Bill's parents also moved back to California soon after we did.

REFLECTION

I believe that water baptism is very important after a person is born again. Peter named it in his discourse on the day of Pentecost as the second thing Christians should do. *"Then Peter said to them, 'Repent, and let every one of you be baptized in the name of Jesus Christ for the remission of sins; and you shall receive the gift of the Holy Spirit.'"* (Acts 2:38 NKJV).

Water baptism does not save us but is necessary to obey the scriptures and it shows our faith in God's Word by our act of obedience. Many times people are filled with the Holy Spirit immediately afterward, but in any case it is symbolic as to what has happened to us spiritually. We are buried with Christ, and arise a *"new creature in Christ Jesus"* (2 Corinthians 5:17). It certainly did that for me and I never wanted to lose that clean feeling I had.

I was so thankful to have Bill's mother as a close-by mentor. She was a wonderful, spirit filled Christian who helped me so much. Everyone needs discipling after being born again, and it's also important to get into a good Bible teaching church.

"Study to shew thyself approved unto God, a workman that needeth not to be ashamed, rightly dividing the word of truth." (2 Timothy 2:15 KJV)

THE SPIRIT OF FEAR

*"For God has not given us a spirit of fear, but
of power and of love and of a sound mind."*
2 Timothy 1:7 NKJV

Fear is one of Satan's greatest tools to use against you. His agenda is to kill, steal and destroy. I learned in a very real way that Fear is a spirit and in itself can kill you.

Bill was working the night shift and usually left about 11:00 pm. My habit had been that after getting the kids to bed I would sit up and crochet while watching television until he left or soon after. One of my favorite programs was Alfred Hitchcock movies. They are mystery stories designed to create suspense, anxiety, and fear. Anyone that has ever watched them knows what I am talking about. They usually end with a sudden climax that leaves the rest of the story up to your imagination which is something horrible that just happened or is about to happen.

On this particular night I had watched one of his movies, and at the very end this family was inside their home feeling safe, after they had been through a terrible ordeal with a certain man that they now thought was dead. Just as the movie ended, it suddenly showed this same, very gruesome and vengeful looking man, watching them through the window.

When I went to bed, all I could think of was the face of that man watching through the window. I looked out my window. There was a street light that gave off a great deal of light, and lit up the entire front yard of our house. Suddenly, I saw that light begin to go dim until it became absolute darkness, an abnormal darkness that seemed to have a presence you could feel.

As the darkness came through the window it came over my face and began to suffocate me. I tried to struggle and fight against it, but it was stronger than me. I suddenly realized something my mother-in-law had told me once. "If you ever get in trouble and don't know what to do, just begin to plead the blood of Jesus."

I couldn't speak by this time. I was about to pass out, but in my mind I kept saying to myself "the blood of Jesus – the blood of Jesus – the blood of Jesus," over and over. Then, suddenly, as fast as it came, it began to go away and leave me. I turned my head slightly toward the wall of the bedroom, and there was a most beautiful, "dancing light." It seemed to be alive with beautiful, transparent colors that moved in and out. It was the most wondrous thing I have ever seen in my life. It is impossible to absolutely describe it, but it transmitted peace like I have never experienced before nor since.

The next thing I remember it was the next morning and time to get up.

REFLECTION

That experience taught me a great lesson about opening doors for Satan to have access. The Spirit of Fear is very real and can kill us if given an opportunity. Watching those types of movies are definitely door openers. To this day, I won't watch anything of the nature that creates fear.

Even if it is just the news or a documentary and I sense that something horrible is about to happen or be shown, I will get up quickly and leave the room. I'm a very visual person; things remain in my head long after I have seen them, especially in the night hours when you are trying to get to sleep.

Parents should be careful about allowing their children to watch such things as well. Many children wake up in the middle of the night screaming because of bad dreams, or nightmares, etc. A lot of it, if not all, is caused by things they watch on television during the day.

Fear will destroy the Christian's faith. Once fear comes in, faith goes out. When something happens that causes fear, we need to refute it quickly with the Word of God. Fear is believing Satan's lies – faith is believing God's truth. When an illness comes and Satan says we're going to die – God says we're going to live and declare the glory of God! Which would you rather have? – Which will you choose? – life or death?

GROWING IN THE WORD

❦

"My people are destroyed for lack of knowledge:"
Hosea 4:6a KJV

Back in California, I had to make new Christian friends, and find another church home. Being a young Christian I didn't use a lot of wisdom concerning my husband. I'm sure he felt "left out" of my life and neglected. We continued to drift further apart. He was bitter about church and didn't like the "new" me.

For the next three years we moved from one small town to another, following his work, so I went to a lot of various churches. He was a heavy duty equipment mechanic through the Operating Engineers Union, and worked on road jobs and dams, anywhere that the job required big equipment.

Kathy, my second child had epileptic seizures from the time she was about three months old, and had to be on medication. Her seizures were still not controlled; I had her prayed for several times but the seizures continued. One night in church I felt very strongly that God had healed her. The next morning I took her medication and threw it in the furnace. She was a little lethargic for a couple of days, but began to seem much better. She became more active than she had ever been. She smiled, played with other children, which she hadn't done before, and I was rejoicing over her healing. Even the neighbors commented on how Kathy had changed, and inquired what had happened? Nearly two years went by without any seizures or medication.

It was time to move on again, and during the drive, Kathy had a seizure. Not having learned how to stand on God's Word in adverse times and circumstances, I immediately said, "Oh no, I guess God didn't heal her after all. We will have to get her to a doctor and get her some more medicine." I came to regret those words for the rest of my life.

Many times I have had Kathy prayed for, and tried to believe God again for her healing, but nothing seemed to work. I finally came to the place where I either had to say that God doesn't heal, and give up, or what…? I knew I couldn't deny my Lord and all that He had done for me to this point, so I finally said "God, I don't understand this right now, but I know you are my savior and healer. I have to put this matter on the shelf until I know more, or you give me wisdom as to what to do." I knew I needed to quit fretting over it, and get on with serving and trusting Jesus. I thought to myself "There is nowhere else to go! He is the only one that has the Words of eternal life and is the only way to the Father." I felt like Peter must have felt when he came to the same conclusion.

"From that time many of His [Jesus'] disciples went back and walked with Him no more. Then Jesus said to the twelve, 'Do you also want to go away?' But Simon Peter answered Him, 'Lord, to whom shall we go? You have the words of eternal life. Also we have come to believe and know that You are the Christ, the Son of the living God.'"
(John 6:66-70 NKJV)

REFLECTION

Many times people don't realize how powerful the words are that come out of their mouth. Our words should always agree with the Word of God. Negative words will bring about negative results, just as God's Word will bring about good results.

"Death and life are in the power of the tongue: and they that love it shall eat the fruit thereof." (Proverbs 18:21)

I should never have confessed that God had not healed Kathy, because it is contrary to God's Word. It is very clear in the scripture that God is our healer.

"But he was wounded for our transgressions, He was bruised for our iniquities: the chastisement of our peace was upon Him; and with His stripes we are healed." (Isaiah 53:5)

I am also reminded of what David said in Psalm 103:1-3

"Bless the Lord, O my soul: and all that is within me, bless his holy name. Bless the Lord, O my soul, and forget not all his benefits: Who forgiveth all thine iniquities; who healeth all thy diseases."

It's always right to agree with the Word of God. Even if we don't "feel" like something is true; His Word is truth and cannot fail. When we confess what the Word says, we are agreeing with God.

LEGALISM

৩৯৫

"For by grace you have been saved through faith,
and that not of yourselves; it is the gift of God,
not of works, lest anyone should boast."
Ephesians 2:8-9 NKJV

After about three years in California, we met some people from Missouri, and decided to move there when they returned home. Bill's parents and sister, along with her two children followed them back, and we moved there a few months later. This would prove to be one of the most miraculous eras of my life.

We ended up in a small community called Abesville, in Stone County. It had one general store and a gas pump out front, and there was one small school house that went to the eighth grade. We parked our trailer just across the street from the general store that had water and gas hook-ups, but it wasn't a trailer park. Our trailer was 8' wide, and 35' long, a two-bedroom, and we had three children by this time. It was actually very comfortable and I was very content in it, even when my sister-in-law with her two kids moved in with us for a few months. We all got along well, even though we had head-to-feet kids doubled up on bunk beds and a hide-a-bed in the living room. We were allowed to use a very old, run-down, empty house next door, that I had wallpapered, painted inside, and cleaned up for the kids to play in during the winter months.

Abesville was about seven miles from Galena, where there was an Assembly of God Church, so we started attending there. Soon I was teaching a Sunday School class, was the church secretary, and led the worship service from time to time. It was a very small church, so there were lots of opportunities for someone anxious to serve. My mother-in-law also taught in the Sunday School and played the piano.

This church happened to be a very *"do's and don'ts church,"* and one of the first things they did was have everyone that was serving, sign a card stating that they would never play cards, go to movies, and several other things that I've forgotten. It didn't bother me, because I didn't have time for any of those things anyway.

Well, the devil knows just how to make things a mess. My husband and I had never gone to a movie since our first year of marriage, but there was a drive-in at another nearby town and he suggested that we take the kids and go one night. I felt terrible, but I remembered the card I had signed and told him I couldn't go and why. This was just one more wedge to come between us. I can see that now, but I thought I was doing the right thing at the time. Signing that card became a real burden to me, even later, and the Lord eventually taught me a great lesson in that matter. It was called "legalism."

REFLECTION

Since that time I have learned that we do not have to add or agree to a lot of rules and works to make our salvation complete. Jesus did it all, once and for all, when He shed His own blood at Calvary. He was our sacrificial lamb. He paid the price for all mankind that we might go free. We just have to receive it and trust in Him. When he said "It is finished," it was complete. When we sign a card or agreement not to do something to make us in right standing, it is legalism and God is not pleased with it. It puts people in bondage and Jesus came to set us free. It was His shed blood alone that cleansed us from all sin, not anything we have done or can do. *"and the blood of Jesus Christ His Son cleanseth us from all sin."* (1 John 1:7b KJV)

SIGNS, WONDERS, AND MIRACLES

*"God also bearing them witness, both with signs
and wonders, and with divers miracles, and gifts
of the Holy Ghost, according to his own will?"*
Hebrews 2:4 KJV

By this time, after attending the Assembly of God Church for about a year, I had met quite a few other people in the community, one of them was a woman about my age, who was engaged to a man that was a Christian, but she was not saved. I had an opportunity to talk to her a lot about the Lord. He went to a different church than we did and actually, our church forbid any of us to go there, saying "it was just a lot of wild fire and of the devil."

One morning, she came by and very excitedly told me she got saved the night before at their church. Her face was absolutely aglow with excitement, it reminded me of my own personal experience. She wanted me to go with her to the next evening service. I wanted to encourage her and go with her, but I again was bound by the admonition from my church to never go to that "wild fire" church. Suddenly, I realized there was something wrong here. How could I be led by the Spirit when all these rules kept preventing me from doing what my heart felt was okay.

After much prayer, I made my decision. It was Saturday. I gathered up all the church books, called the Pastor and made an appointment to see him. When I got there I handed him the church books and resigned from all my duties at the church, telling him to please tear up the card that I had signed. I decided to go with my friend to her church to visit. I couldn't conscientiously do it behind their back. He didn't say much or even try to talk me out of it, so I went.

Before I went, I prayed earnestly, asking the Lord to please protect me from getting into something that might not be right or was not of Him. I asked Him to give me some kind of sign whether He was in that place or not.

It was a small country church somewhere in Stone County, southwest of Springfield, Missouri. Most of the people may not have had any more than an eighth grade education and many not even that much. One woman explained to me that no matter what they taught in school, she had proof that the earth was square and not round, because the Bible speaks of the "four corners of the earth." In spite of their education, they knew how to worship God and they were mightily blessed.

I sat right up front with my friend in the small choir area to the left of the platform. Everything started happening right away. The music was extremely anointed with guitars, banjos, fiddles and more; the pastor played a tambourine. I had never been anywhere like it in my life. I was a little concerned at first, and I just started asking God to show me if all this was real and from Him. In just seconds the anointing fell on me and I began praying in tongues, and I knew it was the Holy Spirit.

Later in the service, I learned that revival broke out in that little church, when a woman in their congregation had begun to fast and pray for her niece that was in the hospital and not expected to live. She had been fasting for about three weeks, and others had been praying also.

People began falling under the power of God everywhere in the room, others testifying of their healings, others crying at the altar and calling on God for salvation.

They had started a nightly revival and I went again the next night. This time, I was again sitting up in the choir area, but was in the back row against the wall. This woman, who had been fasting and praying began to lay hands on people. I was also praying and had my eyes closed, but I soon felt a heat coming towards me and I knew it was from her. The closer she got the hotter it was, and I began to get weak like jelly. I fell down in my chair and pressed up against the wall. I remember thinking "Lord, if she touches me, I'll die." I wasn't afraid, it was just a matter of fact. However, when she did touch me, I felt a surge of power go through me like I'd never before or since experienced. It started from the tips of my fingers and went through me like it was searching out every cell in my body. I could feel it travel all through my body, from one hand and finger tips to the other side, then to my head, and down to the tips of my toes. I leaped to my feet, and felt like I could go through the ceiling. My eyes were still closed, so I can't even say what was happening elsewhere in the room, I felt high above everything else and was standing in the very presence of God, and I didn't want to come back. It was the greatest experience of peace and love that I had never known before.

The next night, the pastor asked me if I would come up and give my testimony from the night before. When I got up to the pulpit they were singing a song that I had never heard before, but the words I will never forget – *"Well, if I could I surely would – stand on that rock where Moses stood – crying Holy to the Lord – crying Holy to*

45

the Lord." I was suddenly in God's presence again, like I had been the night before. I hadn't even opened my mouth yet, when I began to feel my feet moving. My first reaction was that my feet are moving, and I don't know why, so I will just stop.

When I relaxed, thinking I was going to stop them from moving, I took off spinning like a whirlwind. I was totally relaxed, not a tense muscle in my body. In fact, it was like I was in a total resting state. There was a small space between the musicians and the altar bench below the platform, about a couple of feet wide at the most. While spinning, I realized I was going in that direction and becoming more horizontal like I was going to fall and I remembered the narrow space. With my eyes closed, I didn't worry since I was totally relaxed and trusted the Holy Spirit, Who was in complete control. I suddenly flew through that narrow space to about half-way out in the aisle in the middle of the room, never hitting anything. I was thinking "Well, I will probably hit the floor hard," but just inches from the floor, I felt invisible hands under my head, bracing my fall, and eased me to the floor without even the slightest impact. I believe that if I could have seen into the spirit world, there were many, many angels in that little church that night. I think some of them must have been spinning me earlier and another one caught me.

REFLECTION

I had asked God to show me if He was in that place, and He did beyond my greatest expectations. It's always wonderful to hear from God, or be in His presence, and experience the anointing of the Power of God in our physical bodies. I don't believe there is any greater experience on earth than to be in God's presence or hear His voice.

There is one danger though, that we need to be constantly aware of, and that is that Satan always tries to counterfeit everything God does. We should never seek out miracles and signs and wonders. We first need to seek God's face and truth through His Word.

The Bible warns us that the anti-Christ will also come with great lying signs and wonders. If we begin to seek after signs, Satan will be more than glad to accommodate us.

"Even him, whose coming is after the working of Satan with all power and signs and lying wonders." 2 Thessalonians 2:9 KJV

We need to test all manifestations and prophecy with the Word of God. They must line up.

One thing I know is that Satan's greatest weapon is creating fear in people. Fear always negates faith. If he can make you afraid, it gives him the upper hand in your life. Sometimes God warns us in a dream or through prophecy of impending danger, but this gives us an opportunity to pray; we are not to fear, but we need to pray. Prayer changes what Satan has in store for us, and gives God permission to intervene on our behalf.

DECEPTION

*"For there shall arise false Christs, and false prophets,
and shall shew great signs and wonders; insomuch that,
if it were possible, they shall deceive the very elect."*
Matthew 24:24 KJV

One other incident happened during the revival meetings at that small country church that I attended; it was a very valuable lesson about making sure to know the difference in God's voice and another voice. (Satan also attends church at times.)

When I was praying one night during the service, I was on my knees and making a fresh dedication and commitment to the Lord, saying things like "I'll go anywhere you want me to go, do anything you want me to do…" Suddenly a voice spoke to me and said "Will you leave your husband, and children and go preach the gospel for my sake?" It was like somebody threw a bucket of cold water over me; I got up slowly.

As I sat down in my chair I said, "God, is that you?"... just silence, so I said, "I have to think on this." I remember wondering, at the time, if those words were the same ones my mother heard when she was young; I felt they had been. She left my father and all of us when I was about five years old and my younger brother was about three months old. She said God had called her to go preach the gospel. I had always defended her when people talked about her, because she was my mother. Now I had to make a decision, was she right or wrong? I was now faced with the same choice.

The first thing I did the next morning was look up the scripture to see exactly how it read.

> *"... There is no man that hath left house, or brethren, or sisters, or father, or mother, or wife, or children, or lands, for my sake, and the gospel's, but he shall receive an hundredfold now in this time, houses, and brethren, and sisters, and mothers, and children, and lands, with persecutions; and in the world to come eternal life."* (Mark 10:29-30)

Wow, it really sounded like what I had heard. I began to pray about it and asked God to show me what to do. This was really a difficult decision to make, because I wanted to be obedient to God. Somehow, I didn't feel it was from God, because it "just didn't feel and sound right," even though the scripture was very similar.

I thought about my children, I couldn't imagine someone else raising them. How would I know they were getting the right teaching. Then there was also Kathy who needed a lot of special help as well. I had read somewhere in the Bible that said something like, *"Train up a child in the way he should go: and when he is old, he will not depart from it."* (Proverbs 22:6 KJV). I thought, "How can I do that if I'm not here." The Word doesn't contradict itself, so this scripture about leaving must have a deeper meaning that does not apply to my circumstances.

I also tried to picture what the first step in leaving would be, where would I go, how would I begin such a ministry? Nothing seemed clear; I decided to wait on God and do nothing until He gave me some clear direction and instructions. I felt more, and more that I needed to stay with my children. I, long ago, had accepted the fact that I don't understand everything concerning spiritual things, but I did know God's voice, and if something didn't sound like Him, I'd better leave it alone, at least for the time being.

"My sheep hear my voice, and I know them, and they follow me:" (John 10:27)

REFLECTION

We can never let the things we own, whether houses, lands, comforts of life, family members, or anything else stand in the way of following after Christ. That does not mean we have to leave home, unless our life is in danger.

We don't have to physically leave anyone to follow Christ. We have to determine though, that if someone is standing in our way of following Christ, we need to be willing to leave that person (or thing), if necessary. There are places in the world today that if a person confesses Jesus as Lord, they are disowned by their families, or killed if they don't leave home, and sometimes, even sought after and killed if they do leave.

The teachings of Paul to the Ephesians show us how normal family relationships should be.

"For this reason a man shall leave his father and mother and be joined to his wife, and the two shall become one flesh." This is a great mystery, but I speak concerning Christ and the church. Nevertheless let each one of you in particular so love his own wife as himself, and let the wife see that

51

she respects her husband. Children, obey your parents in the Lord, for this is right. "Honor your father and mother," which is the first commandment with promise: "that it may be well with you and you may live long on the earth." And you, fathers, do not provoke your children to wrath, but <u>bring them up in the training and admonition of the Lord.</u>" [emphasis added] (Ephesians 5:31-6:4 NKJV)

The scripture also says *"Train up a child in the way he should go: and when he is old, he will not depart from it."* (Proverbs 22:6)

Both of the above scriptures talk about training our children. How can a parent train up their children, if they are not with them?

No one has to leave anyone to follow after Christ, unless their life is in danger. We are witnesses by our very existence. The light and life of God is in us, and those in darkness will be drawn to the light. By staying with them, who knows that we might lead them to Christ?

"Then Jesus spoke to them again, saying, "I am the light of the world. He who follows Me shall not walk in darkness, but have the light of life." (John 8:12)

Satan, using scripture either in part or out of context, always comes to Christians with something that sounds like the Word of God. People can be deceived if they don't know the Word of God, and are able to rightly divide it. The scriptures tell us that *"My people are destroyed for lack of knowledge..."* (Hosea 4:6) We need to develop a love for the truth, and always seek it out when in doubt. I believe my mother missed it when she left her family. She never realized all her dreams.

We all make mistakes but God still loves us.

A DEEPER EXPERIENCE

ॐ

*"Therefore leaving the principles of the
doctrine of Christ, let us go on unto perfection;
not laying again the foundation of
repentance from dead works, and of faith
toward God."*
Hebrews 6:1 KJV

My mother-in-law and I continued to attend that "wild-fire" church we had visited on a regular basis, and I began teaching a Sunday School class once again; God was moving in a deeper way in my life.

After my initial experience at that church, with the heat and fire that I experienced, I began to notice a change in my eating habits. After having three children, pretty close together, I had put on a little excess weight, and had developed some bad eating habits. I was about 26 at the time. The first thing I noticed was that I no longer had a desire for a soda during the day, but about mid-day or so I drank a glass of milk. I had always disliked milk and was told I was allergic to it. I no longer had a desire for junk food, but my eating habits changed, and over a month's time, I lost weight without dieting. People

53

began to comment about it, and it opened the door to testify about what God had done.

REFLECTION

I believe when I was touched with the Holy Spirit in such a supernatural way, that everything within me was "made physically whole." If I had any disease, either minor or major, I was completely healed; nothing adverse in our bodies can remain under the mighty power of God. He changes our desires, our dreams, and our very being to become more in line with His will.

Being in His presence was the most glorious experience I ever received. As I have meditated on this since then, I realize that God is one hundred percent "Love." No one on earth has ever experienced that kind of love. I think we are going to be amazed at what "super-great" things are in store for us when we get "home." The things of this world cannot begin to be compared with what God has in store for us. That one experience alone made that very real to me.

WALKING IN OBEDIENCE

"How is it then, brethren? When ye come together, every one of you hath a psalm, hath a doctrine, hath a tongue, hath a revelation, hath an interpretation. Let all things be done unto edifying."
1 Corinthians 14:26 KJV

The Bible began to be even more alive to me. One day, as I was reading the scripture in John 12:24-27, God revealed it to me in a new and deeper way.

"Verily, verily, I say unto you, except a corn of wheat fall into the ground and die, it abideth alone: but if it die, it bringeth forth much fruit. He that loveth his life shall lose it; and he that hateth his life in this world shall keep it unto life eternal. If any man serve me, let him follow me; and where I am, there shall also my servant be: if any man serve me, him will my Father honour. Now is my soul troubled; and what shall I say? Father, save me from this hour: but for this cause came I unto this hour." (John 12:24)

55

God gave me some very specific insights into the meaning of this scripture, and then told me I was going to give the message on this scripture at the little church next door that night. It was a week night and they only held services one night a week, when they had a preacher available. I had planned to attend, but didn't know many of the people. Since it was so close, I thought I would try it. I didn't even know how they believed, or what denomination they were; I couldn't imagine them asking me to speak, but I was ready, because I knew God's voice, and I wanted to obey.

I didn't know anyone there, and was a fairly timid person, so I sat in the very back row. They sang some songs, and after a little while a man stood up and said something to the effect that the preacher couldn't make it tonight, some car trouble or something. Then he proceeded to ask if anyone had a scripture, a message or any comments they would like to share. I knew that was my cue since the Lord had told me I was to speak. I was petrified and almost didn't raise my hand, but I knew I had to. Finally, when he almost proceeded to close the meeting, my hand suddenly shot up and I said "I have a scripture."

I walked up to the pulpit and was so nervous. I remembered they usually pray before speaking, so I said "Let's pray." That helped me immensely, and then I was calm and asked everyone to turn to the scripture God had given me.

After making the comments the Lord had given me, and the service was dismissed, a young woman came up to me and thanked me for the message. She said it was just what she needed and it meant so much to her. I think I realized, at that moment, that when we come to church with a need and expect something from God, He will raise up someone to meet the need of that person – *if everyone is obedient.*

REFLECTION

I always try to encourage people to attend church faithfully as the Bible admonishes us. We don't have to be the preacher to have a word of encouragement for someone.

"And let us consider one another in order to stir up love and good works, not forsaking the assembling of ourselves together, as is the manner of some, but exhorting one another, and so much the more as you see the Day approaching." (Hebrews 10:24-25 NKJV)

We all need encouragement from time to time. You might be the one God will use to speak a word to meet someone's need that night, whether it be in the pulpit, the lobby, on the sidewalk outside, or in the parking lot.

One of my greatest encounters was with an individual I met on the sidewalk between the two buildings at church. All I said was "Hi, how are you?" and slowed down walking to let her know I really wanted to know. She first said "fine," but then said, "no, I'm not fine," then just exploded in my arms in tears as she began to pour her heart out. God met us gloriously and she left with a smile on her face, thanking God as she went.

Always be prayed up, available and obedient to the leading of the Holy Spirit.

LETTING GO

"For he shall give his angels charge over thee, to keep thee in all thy ways. They shall bear thee up in their hands, lest thou dash thy foot against a stone."
Psalm 91:11-12 KJV

By this time Billy, my oldest child, was in school and it was time to start thinking about Kathy going to school. In addition to the seizures, Kathy still had some very challenging problems. Her doctor had told me that she had brain damage at birth. We had been taking her to a speech therapist, and even though I could understand everything she said, other people couldn't. There were certain combinations of letters that she just could not pronounce correctly. The doctor told me that I should not try to send her to school, it might push her over the edge and create more problems, making things even worse. He said it would be impossible for her to learn to read or do simple arithmetic.

It just happened that the school teacher for the lower grades lived a couple of houses to the left of us, and she asked me about Kathy. When I told her what the doctor had said, she asked me to please send her to school because she wanted to work with her. I thought it wouldn't hurt to give it a try. If she felt it was impossible for her to learn we would understand, and just take her out of school.

This brought up another issue; she would have to ride the school bus. The night before her first day of school, I began to imagine all kinds of things that could happen to her. She might have a seizure when starting to get on the bus and fall under the wheels, or when going up the steps to the school house she might have a seizure and fall off the stairs under the rail. Then I thought about the school swings and many other episodes where she might be in danger. I prayed and sought God nearly all night about what to do. Finally, near morning, God spoke to me and made me to realize that I could not be with her every moment for the rest of her life, to watch over her, but He could. His angels would be with her every minute of the day protecting her. It gave me such peace. By morning, I was okay with letting her go to school.

After a couple of months in school, her teacher told me that Kathy was still having trouble learning to read. I decided to see whether I could help her. So we got her reader out and I noticed that she knew some of the words, but the first thing I noticed was that she wanted to call every word that started with a capital "M" Mother. When she got to "Mary" she called it "Mother." After questioning her further, I observed that she thought each letter was a word, and she had simply memorized some of the other words from hearing them. When I told her that it took all of the letters in the word "Mother" to make up the word, and not just the first letter; suddenly her face lit up. She got it. She soon learned to sound out her letters and caught up to the rest of her class in no time.

60

REFLECTION

I have thought much about our guardian angels and the protection God promised me concerning Kathy. Angels are ministering spirits sent by God to help those that are to inherit salvation.

"But to which of the angels has He ever said: "Sit at My right hand, till I make your enemies your footstool"? Are they not all ministering spirits sent forth to minister for those who will inherit salvation?" (Hebrews 1:13-14)

When Jesus was In the Garden of Gethsemane, and the soldiers came for him, Jesus said to them: *"Or do you think that I cannot now pray to My Father, and He will provide Me with more than twelve legions of angels?"* (Matthew 26:53) I believe there were angels standing by, even when he was on the cross, hoping to be sent, but we know the story, that Jesus had to bear the shame, and sins, alone, for our redemption. This tells us that angels must be sent from God. They could not go to Jesus' aid of their own free will. We cannot ask angels to protect us; we must pray and ask God to protect us. The angels are just the ministering spirits that God sends.

The scripture in Psalm 34:7 tells us: *"The angel of the Lord encampeth round about them that fear him, and delivereth them."*

There are times when I know angels helped me when I didn't even know I was in danger, but when we're in the family of God, I believe they watch over us always as God directs them.

When we really put our complete trust in God and walk according to His Word, we can apply such scriptures to our lives, knowing that God's angels are always all around us to deliver us. We just have to cry out *"HELP!"*

61

FASTING

❧❧

*"And Jesus said to them, 'Can the friends of
the bridegroom mourn as long as the bridegroom
is with them? But the days will come when the
bridegroom will be taken away from
them, and then they will fast.'"*
Matthew 9:15 NKJV

On one occasion, I felt led to fast and pray to draw closer to the Lord. On the second night of the fast, Lynn, who was about three years old at the time, suddenly became very ill; she had a high fever and was shaking. I contemplated for a moment about taking her to the hospital in Springfield, but it would be an hour's drive over a very rough road (some of it dirt) in to Springfield. It was the middle of the night, my tires were bad, my other kids were asleep, and Bill had to go to work the next morning. Cell phones were unheard of in those days, so I asked God what should I do, and began to pray for her. After a few minutes her fever broke and she seemed okay. She soon went back to sleep. The next morning, she was fine. I guess I will never know what was wrong with her, but God took care of it.

The third night of no food *or water*, I had a vision. I was lying on the bed gazing out the window when suddenly, a black screen just scrolled across the window and I saw a beautiful sunset with saguaro cactus and mountains; a very familiar scene to me, since I was originally from Phoenix, Arizona. Suddenly, there appeared a very depraved and troubled man, looking up as if from hell itself. I knew from the vision that I would be going back to Arizona, but had no idea who the man was. I felt it was someone I would meet there. Also, one night I heard my father's voice call me. He was the only one that always called me "Anna." I could never mistake his voice. It woke me up, out of a deep sleep, and it was so real that I got up and walked through the house to see if somehow he was there. It seemed like another sign to me that I would be going home, but I didn't know how it would be possible. I knew God would work things out, in His time.

REFLECTION

Fasting is something the church leaders in Jesus' day did as part of their ritual to let people see how spiritual they were. The Lord told us how we are to fast:

> *"Moreover, when you fast, do not be like the hypocrites, with a sad countenance. For they disfigure their faces that they may appear to men to be fasting. Assuredly, I say to you, they have their reward. But you, when you fast, anoint your head and wash your face, so that you do not appear to men to be fasting, but to your Father who is in the secret place; and your Father who sees in secret will reward you openly."* (Matthew 6:16-18 NKJV)

There are times when it seems like our prayers just don't seem to reach above our head, and we feel we need to draw closer to God. There are many reasons why a Christian may choose to fast. It is not a rule or ritual that gives us more points with God; however, it does bring our flesh under subjection, and our spiritual man becomes stronger. There is power in fasting, but not because God is impressed with our sacrifice. Jesus did not say His disciples did not need to fast, but "when you fast…" By this we know it is scriptural to fast. When the disciples could not cast out the demon in the case of the epileptic child, he said to His disciples *"This kind can come out by nothing but prayer and fasting."* (Mark 9:29) NKJV I have never gone on a three-day fast <u>without water</u> since that time. Most of the time people are led only to a "no food" fast.

[Note: Depravation of water for a very long period of time can be very serious and you should be certain God leads you into it.]

DESPERATE TIMES

"But whoever has this world's goods, and sees his brother in need, and shuts up his heart from him, how does the love of God abide in him?"
1 John 3:17 NKJV

Living conditions had become very difficult, but we had an opportunity to make a trade for ten acres of land with a good, natural spring on it. We didn't have to pay rent anymore, it was beautiful country and we had a wonderful garden that produced a tremendous bounty of food, some of which we traded for milk and other things we couldn't grow. I separated the cream off the top of the milk and churned it to make butter. I also learned to can food for the winter months. The men went fishing in the James River, catching mostly carp, which I canned. Most people would not eat it, because it had so many bones, but it provided good protein, and along with the fresh garden vegetables, made for very healthy, nourishing meals. (When the fish is canned, the bones crumble just like canned salmon and you can use it in all kinds of recipes.)

There was no work in the area. Bill and his father had a welding and mechanic shop right next door to the General Store, but most of the people wanted to trade food or other items for their work. Many times Bill would come home with less than $5 a week. You can't pay your electric bill by trading. That was the only bill we had, and we were having a hard time paying it. I got a job at the local newspaper in Galena, making $35 a week for a short time, until we moved to Kansas.

By this time, I was about seven months pregnant with Barbara. It was winter time and we rented a house in the country where the wind whipped through intensely. It was always freezing cold and all we could do was try to stay warm. I brought all the beds into the large living room and circled them around the only stove in the huge, rambling house. Some of the rooms we just completely closed off to try to keep the living room and kitchen warm. In the kitchen I turned the stove up as high as possible and opened the oven door to try to stay warm.

Bill was a traveling salesman trying to sell Britannica Encyclopedias. He sold one or two sets, but not enough to pay our bills. We finally found a place in town that had a good heater and we could be warm. The kids went to school for a couple of weeks, but soon we were out of food and money. I didn't have food to pack their lunch, so I just kept them home. Lynn was not in school yet. By now, I was about 8-1/2 months pregnant with Barbara; I never felt so helpless in my life. In times past, I would figure some way to earn some money, but physically, now, it was impossible.

I didn't know what to do, so when I went to church one Sunday, I told the pastor my story, and that we desperately needed help. We had no food left in the house and I had no milk for my children. It was a very large church and I had only been attending there about two or three weeks, since we moved into town. He said he would pray for me and the Lord would provide.

I came home so devastated and kept trying to think of what to do. The next door neighbor had a couple of small children and asked if Billy and Kathy could spend the rest of the day over there with her kids. I thought she would probably feed them at least, so I let them go.

While they were gone I remember sitting down in my rocking chair, trying to think about what I was going to do. I couldn't contact my husband (no cell phones or any way to get in touch with him). I didn't know for sure where he was, but I knew where his boss lived, and even though he wasn't home either, his wife was. She always seemed to know how to get in touch with her husband. We had become good friends.

Suddenly, I began to feel dizzy and faint. I couldn't remember what I was supposed to be doing or where my children were. It was a very panicky feeling, but I made it to the couch where the phone was, and strangely enough I remembered Marilyl's phone number (the wife of Bill's boss). When she picked up the phone, I remember just saying something like "I need help. I can't remember anything." Then I fainted, still holding the phone. She didn't have a car, nor did she drive, but she had called a taxi and the next thing I knew she was waking me up. She said she was taking me to the doctor and had the taxi driver wait. I couldn't remember how to go about doing anything, or even where the bedroom or bathroom was. She guided me from room to room and had to tell me everything to do to get ready. By the time we got to the doctor's office, after waiting about an hour, I slowly began to remember things. My dad later said I had temporary amnesia from over-worrying, and the mind, in an attempt to protect itself, goes into a "pause" mode to keep from snapping completely. My dad seemed to always know everything, and whether he was right or wrong, I always believed whatever he told me. The doctor said my husband needed to be contacted and I needed to be under a doctor's care regularly until the baby came.

Marilyl's husband contacted my husband and he came home immediately with a trailer behind his truck. We loaded up everything that night and headed back for Missouri the next morning.

In about two more weeks, Barbara was born in Springfield, Missouri. After coming home, things were still very hard; I didn't have money for milk, diapers, or any of the very basic things we needed. A decision had to be made; Bill didn't want to leave there because his mother, father and sister lived there.

Bill's and my relationship was no longer as important as my children's needs. I felt I had to do something to protect my children. We had already run up a $250 bill at the general store, buying groceries and other necessary items. I could no longer walk in the place and ask for more, not knowing how I was ever going to pay them.

Finally, I picked up the phone one day, and called my father. I said "Dad, this ship is sinking, and I and the kids want to get off. Can I borrow $200 to come home." He not only sent me the $200, but also his credit card. Barbara was five months old at this time, and it was early November.

On the day I left, when Bill got home for lunch, I had the big Packard packed to the hilt, with a portable playpen fixed in the back seat for Barbara and room for Billy to sit next to it, so he could watch her. Kathy and Lynn sat in the front seat with me. I took as many of their clothes as possible, and the only other thing I took, other than some of my clothes, was my sewing machine which fit in the trunk. Packards had huge trunks. We were ready to go.

I told Bill, "I'm leaving for Arizona. You can have everything we own, I don't want anything, I'm not divorcing you, I'm just leaving, because my children are not going to starve and live like this. You can follow me if you like, or you can stay here. I'm not mad at you. I don't hate you. We're just getting out of here." I got in the car with the kids and drove off.

It was an old car and since Bill was a mechanic, it was probably in fair condition. I never worried about it. I trusted God to watch over us. The tires were bald, but I had a spare and could change a tire in no time. I made sure I had tire-changing tools. The roads were icy along the way, and there were places we went through where it was snowing or raining, but overall the trip was pretty much fun for all of us. The kids had never been on a long road trip, and they were excited about going to Arizona. To make the trip easier, I bought some disposable diapers for Barbara, the first I had ever used for any of my kids.

I drove non-stop to Albuquerque, except for necessary "pit stops." We got a motel room there for the night, since we had left late in the day, and I had driven all night, I didn't have to fix or stop for any meals. I had packed sandwiches and enough food to eat in the car; the kids were exceptionally good.

None of the kids had ever been in a motel before, and although I had always fought with Billy to take a bath at home, he could hardly wait to take a bath in the motel. There was a small divider between the two bed areas. It was nice and warm and we all went right off to sleep with no incidents.

The next morning, we headed out again, but I barely got across a small bridge headed out of town, after leaving the service station, when my car suddenly stopped. I pulled over and noticed a truck in the field next to the road. I called out to the man in the truck and he came to the fence to see what I wanted. I told him that my car quit running and was there any way he could call a tow truck or help us get back to the service station. He came

Barbara - 4 mos.

Lynn - 4 yrs.

Ann with Barbara, Billy, Lynn, & Kathy
General store in Abesville, Missouri, just before moving
back to Arizona

over, saw the situation, and took us all back to the service station in his truck and sent someone for the car.

When we got gas earlier, the attendant had told me we needed a new hose for the fuel pump, so I had them put one on. When we got back to the station, they looked at the car to see what was wrong. The person that had put the hose on forgot to screw it down, and the nut was still lying right next to it on a cross bar (Thank you, Jesus!). It was a miracle that it hadn't rolled off. He screwed it back on, got things working again, and didn't charge us anything.

The gasoline attendant had also told me that I desperately needed new tires. He didn't think I would ever make it to Phoenix on the bald tires we had, and it was also very dangerous. I didn't want to spend any more of Dad's money than I had to, so I just said I would take a chance with what we had. I knew God was with us and had no fear. I knew He would take care of us. Not only did I make it in to Phoenix without any more problems, but I drove an additional two years on those tires before finally getting new ones.

Bill always said I was living proof that people have guardian angels. "The way you drive across country, or anywhere you decide to go in an old rattle-trap car and always get by is absolutely incredible." I believe that sometimes *not knowing* what's under the hood of a car or how dangerous something can be, allowed me to have more faith in God's protection. I always knew He was with me wherever I was. I felt I was as safe in one place, as I was in another.

REFLECTION

I know God's angels followed us and surrounded us on that trip. I will probably never know the many times they kept us from dangerous situations. We had an old

73

car, bad tires, four small children and no serious incidents the entire trip.

I can look back and see God's hand of protection and provision over us in so many ways. There was the friend I had in Kansas to help get me to a doctor and notify my husband. Then there were the people in the general store that gave us credit when we were so desperate and had nothing. When I called my dad, he was able to help when I desperately needed it. Then there was the man in the pickup truck in the field nearby when our car died. There were no other cars or anyone anywhere, but there he was, in the middle of nowhere, just across the fence when our car stopped. There were the caring people at the service station along the way. And, I'm certain God's angels were always nearby. Some of those people may have even been angels.

God works through people – don't miss an opportunity to be used by Almighty God when such an occasion arises. There are a lot of people that are always asking for help; many times we fail to take advantage of the opportunities that come along to bless someone else. We need to use discretion about what is helpful; however, I decided a few years ago that instead of trying to figure out if people are lying or cheating, it is always better, and I believe more pleasing to God, to err on the side of doing good, than to withhold when there could possibly be a real need. Let God be the judge!

You may think you don't have enough to help, but if you ask God to show you how you can help, I believe you will be surprised at the things the Holy Spirit will bring to your mind. The first step is to be willing, and I can almost guarantee that God will use you.

TRUSTING GOD FOR THE FUTURE

❦

*"And those who know Your name will put
their trust in You; for You, Lord, have
not forsaken those who seek you."*
Psalm 9:10 NKJV

I didn't know where we were going from here, but knew God would direct me. My first agenda was, of course, to find a job.

We stayed with my Dad for about two weeks. We had immediately started the kids in school. Kathy was in the second grade by this time. She walked to school with Billy, and the plan was that she would also come home with him. Something happened and they either got out at different times or somehow got separated, so she started home on her own. Dad lived in a subdivision where all the houses looked alike and we had not discussed with her the names of streets. Billy got home and no one knew where Kathy was, so we began to go up and down all the streets looking for her. A couple of hours had gone by, and finally, as I started down a certain street, I saw her. When I parked and walked over to her, she didn't cry,

75

Ann's dad, Richard Bagwell
and his wife Marguerite's
wedding picture

1
9
6
3

Billy

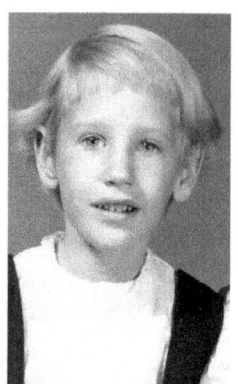

Kathy

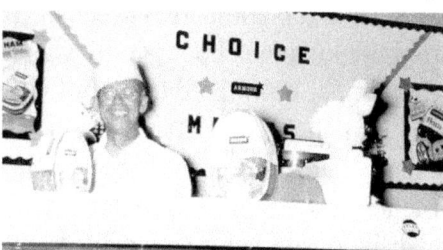

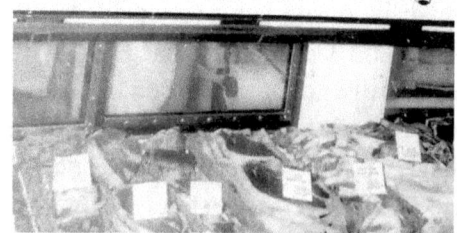

Ann's dad at work in the meat market

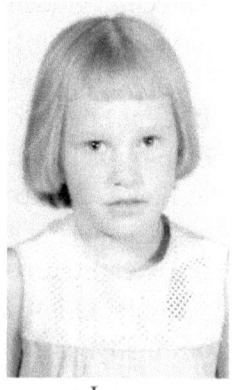

Lynn

but just looked at me with such relief in her eyes, and said "Mom, I'm so glad you found me." It just broke my heart, because I know she had been frightened, not knowing where to go, but Kathy didn't know how to express herself, and never showed much emotion. I thanked God for watching over her once again, and keeping her safe.

During the time we were at my Dad's house, I remember one night when Dad came home from work, he announced that President Kennedy had been shot and was dead. I never saw my Dad so devastated. Being a young mother, I had never been concerned about who was President, and really didn't care at that particular time in my life. Just two weeks in my father's home changed that quickly. Afterwards I began to pay attention, and was a registered voter by the next election.

I only used about $200 of Dad's money (gasoline was about 25 cents a gallon then). I paid him back everything, as soon as I could, which was about six months later.

We were living with Dad and my step-mother, Marguerite, for about two weeks, when I learned that my aunt (one of my mother's sisters) lived about a mile away.

MOVING IN WITH MY AUNT

I had started going to church at the local Assembly of God, and somehow my conversation with the Pastor revealed that my aunt Sudie, one of my mother's sisters, also attended the church there. The last time I had seen her was when I was about 4 years old before my mother left. The Pastor gave me her address and phone number. She lived nearby, and had a large 3-bedroom home. Since she lived alone, she insisted that I bring the kids and come live with her. This was the first contact I had with any of my relatives on my mother's side of the family. This was a miracle in itself, especially in the way it came about and how I was able to get in touch with her. We didn't have the same last name or anything that would indicate we were relatives.

Aunt Sudie was a very sweet woman and anxious to help us. We had no money, and even though I had applied for several jobs, nothing had opened up yet.

It was getting close to Christmas and I hadn't heard anything from Bill, but unknown to me, he had called my Dad looking for me. Dad told him where we were. It was Christmas Eve, and there was nothing for the kids under the tree. My aunt gave me $20 and told me to go to Walgreens on the corner and get something for the kids. They were having special sales every five minutes when I got there, something like K-Mart's blue-light specials.

I came home with several items for each child. It was unbelievable what I got for that $20. My cousin, Charlyn, that also lived nearby, came by and dropped off several toys for the kids, including a BB gun for Billy. They lived on a farm nearby and all her boys had BB guns. She invited us to come over and visit.

That same night, after the kids had gone to bed, there was a knock on the door. It was Bill. He had driven all day and night to get there before Christmas. My aunt was very hospitable and made him feel welcome. It was a happy and joyous evening indeed.

The next day was a beautiful day, and a new beginning for our family. Bill had sold everything we had in Missouri, and was there to stay.

STARTING OVER

Over the next few months, we both had gotten jobs and moved to a 2-bedroom house closer to the center of town, only a few blocks from my half-sister, Kim (at that time known as Grace before she changed her name.)

I had only met her once before in high school. She reminded me a lot of my sister Mary, but I never really got to know her at that time. She and my half-brother "Buddy" were born after my mother left my father and they were raised by my Aunt Mamie, another sister of my mother's, who lived with her seven children at New River, Arizona.

Kim was married to Dan Ginn, at that time, and had two small children, Jim and John, from her previous marriage to Jim Chambers.

When I got a job close by, she insisted on baby-sitting for Barbara. Lynn had just started to school, and all three of the kids went to Kim's house after school until I picked them up. She didn't charge me anything and it gave me a chance to catch up on things and begin to get ahead a little. After Bill and I started working, the very first thing I did was pay my Dad what I owed him, and sent the money to the General Store in Abesville to pay off our $250 debt. I remembered someone had said once, that a person should owe no man anything "but love." I took that seriously, and have always tried to live by that rule.

"Owe no one anything except to love one another, for he who loves another has fulfilled the law." (Romans 13:8 NKJV)

I was still going to church, taking the kids, and paying my tithe. It's a good feeling to pay the tithe when you've been poor for so long, like we had been.

Through everything, God had directed my path, kept us safe, and provided for our needs when we had nothing. It was miraculous to me how everything worked out so well. I can look back and see the hand of God over our family, leading us through it all. It was so good to meet many of my relatives again, and build a relationship with them, as well as, with my Dad and his new wife, Marguerite.

REFLECTION

When I left Missouri, I had no idea what the future would hold, but felt it was something I had to do, and somehow I knew things would work out. My thoughts were that I would get a job, find a reliable baby sitter, and possibly raise my children as a single parent.

When we allow ourselves to be led by the Spirit of God, He is able to work miracles in our lives that we never dreamed possible. Nothing worked out the way I had anticipated but much better in every way. Meeting the other side of my family again was something I never dreamed would happen. Even my father seemed to appreciate what they did for us, and was not bitter towards them, as he had been during our growing up years.

The scripture tells us in Isaiah 58:7 *"Share your food with the hungry, and give shelter to the homeless. Give clothes to those who need them, and do not hide from relatives who need your help."* NLT

I often see people in desperate circumstances and both parents have passed away; they have no other relatives anywhere to help them. I can't even imagine how alone and helpless they must feel. We must always be willing to reach out to such people, and offer them help, as we would want to be helped.

I don't know what I would have done, or what would have happened to us, if my Dad had not responded to my plea for help; then my aunt came along and just made our lives so much more comfortable. God always works beyond our wildest imaginations.

A TRAGIC EXPERIENCE

$\wp \infty \wp$

"And again, I will put my trust in Him. And again,
behold I and the children which God hath given me."
Hebrews 2:13 KJV

While living more in the heart of Phoenix, we had started going to a small church nearby. Kathy was probably in about the 3rd or 4th grade at the time. It was in the summer time and the church had evaporative coolers, as well as fans. While Kathy was going to her Sunday School class one morning, there was a hallway the children passed through, and in a low window nearby was a large fan blowing. It was low enough for a child to just reach out and touch. Kathy was fascinated by it and put her hand towards it out of curiosity. She got her fingers too close, and two of them were nearly cut off.

We grabbed a towel and wrapped around them and rushed her to the nearest hospital, which was Maricopa County hospital. Initially, she just looked shocked and didn't cry or anything. Then when the pain really hit her, she only whimpered a little. Kathy didn't show a lot of emotion and because of that, I didn't feel she got the service and attention she needed. I called my doctor and he had her transferred to another hospital. Within the hour, the personnel at the new hospital cleaned and dressed her wound, and x-rays were taken. She had nearly severed two fingers on her right hand, including cutting through both tendons. They had a hand specialist come in, and after many days in the hospital we were told that she may never have normal use of her hand again.

After the hand healed enough to begin therapy, we were told that she needed to squeeze the little ball they gave her several times a day to help build up strength and hopefully restore the use of her hand. Kathy heard the directions as well, and every time we turned around she was squeezing that ball for months afterwards. As a result, her right hand is probably stronger than a lot of people's, and her fingers work normally.

REFLECTION

In May of 2002, Kathy had a stroke during brain surgery that affected her left side, so her right hand has become even stronger by taking up the slack of doing more with one hand. She has long scars across the top of her fingers, but they aren't real noticeable; no one would ever know that she had ever cut them as badly as she did.

Kathy has been in and out of the hospital so many times in her life, I can't even count them, but we got through them all, and I always knew she would be okay, because of God's promise to me years before. It seems that the devil has tried to kill her from before she was born and ever since. She has survived and bounced back when doctors said she wouldn't.

It seems we always had the very best doctors. After I called our own doctor and had her moved to another hospital, when she had her fingers cut, she got the immediate care she needed. Proper care and knowledge is extremely important in serious conditions, and I believe God has always provided us with the best doctors in every emergency we've been through.

The brain surgery was to remove the portion of her brain that caused the major part of her seizures. We were told it would not eliminate all of them, but it reduced the amount from several times a day to three or five times a month. The stroke however created a new problem; her left arm and leg is paralyzed and she now has to use a walker to help her walk. She just takes it in stride and continues to do all that she can. She is still on medication for her seizures, but not as much as prior to the surgery.

Kathy didn't hear the doctor's prognosis concerning her hands, or understand it, or when the doctor said she wouldn't live to be 30 years old; so she just continued to recover and live. She is now 59 years old. Our mind and attitude has so much to do with how fast our body heals from wounds or disease. I also learned to trust God and His Word more and more. We have to *walk by faith and not by sight* (2 Corinthians 5:7) if we're going to receive God's promises for our life.

Chapter 2

THE MIDDLE YEARS

Left to right: Kathy, Lynn in back, Billy at right,
and Barbara in front

BUILDING ON THE FOUNDATION

"According to the grace of God which was given to me, as a wise master builder I have laid the foundation, and another builds on it. But let each one take heed how he builds on it. For no other foundation can anyone lay than that which is laid, which is Jesus Christ."
1 Corinthians 3:10-11 NKJV

Eventually, we were able to buy a house on the west side of Phoenix, toward Glendale. It was very close to my Dad and my Aunt again.

We met new and lasting friends at that location. Ted and Carol Houck lived on one side of us, and when we drove up to our new home, they were out washing their car. I thought they were two teenagers, perhaps a potential baby-sitter. When I went over to meet them, I asked if her mother was home, and found out she was the mother. They had gotten married very young. She was 16 and he was 17, and she did turn out to be a very good baby-sitter and neighbor and they also went to the same church with us. A few years ago Bob and I went to their 50th wedding anniversary.

Drexel and Betty Pope, Senior pastors of Word Chapel

My life was about to change again with a new and deeper relationship with God. The church we had started going to was a non-denominational, full-gospel church.

The pastor gave all the kids a nickel, if they could come up front and say their memory verses perfectly. Kathy got more nickels than anyone else. She was the first up front every Sunday morning. I didn't realize it then, but later in her life, we discovered that she has a photographic memory. That also explained why she always made 100% on every spelling test.

We met several very good friends there – Betty and Drexel Pope, the Abbotts, the Mendenhalls, the Skeltons, and several others of whose names I've forgotten.

We had been going there for less than a year, when the church disbanded because the pastor left.

Some of the other families, that had been attending, went together to build a church nearby. One of the men in the group was a building contractor, and they all donated their time and money to build a debt-free church. The church was called Word Chapel. Most of the congregation migrated there, since we didn't know where else to go.

The Word of God and the gifts of the Spirit were really emphasized in this church. Drexel Pope, the senior pastor, was very deep in the Word, and the other ministers had many gifts and abilities to offer the body of Christ. They all, interchangeably, ministered from time to time. Betty Pope was a great children's teacher, and taught all the school-age children. Carol Houck, my next door neighbor, taught the pre-school, and managed the nursery.

It was a small congregation but, oh, what power! I and my children really began to grow in the Lord at that little church. Lynn was filled with the Holy Spirit at the age of 9 through the teaching of Betty Pope and her children's ministry. I believe it was her teachings that helped sustain my children later in life. My cousin, Charlyn Robinson and her seven children, also attended Word Chapel, so all of her children and mine got to know each other very well.

Our home life was still not ideal. Bill didn't go to church with us and never made himself a real part of our family. He always had other things to do and places to go.

At times, I would get so frustrated with him. At one particular time, when he did something I felt was totally unreasonable and hateful, I was praying and telling the Lord all about how awful he was and please do something with him. The Lord spoke to me ever so gently and said. "I loved you when you were unlovable." God doesn't have to say very much to get his point across. I never "ragged" on him to the Lord again, but learned to be tolerant and quiet.

REFLECTION

When we purchased our house on the Northwest side of Phoenix, we began to develop more structure and stabilization in our home.

We soon found a good solid church home and probably looked like a pretty normal family to most outsiders.

Bill had taken up flying by this time, so all of his spare time was spent studying or flying. We never talked much, taking our roles in life for granted, not trying to develop our relationship with each other. In our personal life, we drifted farther apart. I wasn't smart enough at that time, and he probably wasn't either, to realize that we were separating from each other; therefore, neither one of us worked at fixing things.

I was busy with the children, going to Brownie meetings, coaching for Lynn's softball team, being a homeroom mother, making all their clothes, shopping, and just normal household chores. When Barbara was in kindergarten, I also drove the school bus and later got a part time job setting type in a book publishing house.

I really don't know what Bill was doing all this time except going to work, coming home, watching TV, and on the weekends flying. We never went anywhere or did anything together. Neither one of us was paying attention or realized that our marriage was in trouble.

Ann's Mother, Mattie Bee

MEETING MY BIOLOGICAL MOTHER

*"There came then his brethren and his mother,
and, standing without, sent unto him, calling him.
And the multitude sat about him, and they said unto
him, Behold, thy mother and thy brethren without seek
for thee. And he answered them, saying, who
is my mother, or my brethren? And he looked round
about on them which sat about him, and said,
behold my mother and my brethren! For whosoever
shall do the will of God, the same is my brother,
and my sister, and mother."*
Mark 3:31-35 KJV

During the years while attending Word Chapel, my biological mother came to visit me one day. She had learned from my cousin where I lived. I welcomed her like I would a stranger and we tried to have a good visit, but it was pretty awkward. She had a small portable typewriter in her car, and asked if she could bring it in to show it to me. "Of course," I said. When she brought it in, she set it up, and asked me to type something for her while she dictated it. As I began typing, I realized that this was something very strange and uncomfortable for me. It was a personal note to my father, as spoken by me, asking him to see my mother; that she was very anxious to see him again and she had never stopped loving him.

I didn't know what her intentions were, and thought she was just trying to let me know how she felt, but then she asked me to sign it and mail it to him. That's when I rebelled, and told her I couldn't possibly do such a thing. He was happily married again and she no longer was any part of his life, so she shouldn't attempt to be. She lashed out at me with such anger, quoting all kinds of scriptures about not honoring her as my mother, condemning me for disobedience; making me feel guilty, and that I needed to repent. The anger went on and on for some time before she finally stormed out the door with her typewriter. I ran to the bedroom and tried to pray. I felt I had done something terrible, and then I said, "Lord I don't understand how this happened. If she's a Christian and I'm a Christian, what are we going to do when we both get to heaven; this is not right."

About that time the doorbell rang, and she was there, ever so sweet and polite. She said something about it was okay for my kids to call her Grandma, if they wanted to. It was like nothing had ever happened. She was so sweet and gushy. I couldn't believe this was the same woman that had just stormed out of my house. She left right away again, and I was more confused than ever, feeling very guilty for the way I had responded to her at the first meeting. I prayed again and asked the Lord to show me about how to handle this new encounter.

No one in our church had ever heard anything about my mother since I never talked about her. She had left the family when I was five years old and I really never knew her.

One night, soon after my meeting with her, I was in church and one of the other ministers, brother Mendenhall, was preaching. Suddenly, he stopped and began to prophesy. He saw open visions of things, and he just began to speak what he was seeing. He said "I see Ann's mother as a young woman, about 18 years old. She is standing outside a church building. She is holding her Bible and now I see a great nervousness come over her and her whole body is beginning to shake. She begins to laugh uncontrollably. She is confused about something in the Bible. She has been holding on to someone's hand, and I see her let go and walk away."

After the service, I went up to him and asked him whose hand she had let go of. He said, almost apologetically, "the hand of Jesus." I didn't know what to think about all this. I knew she had said she left my Dad to go preach the gospel, but later, after my own experience, and after hearing that same voice, I felt like she had listened to "another voice," rather than the voice of God.

REFLECTION

Satan is such a liar and deceiver – nothing ever turns out well when we listen to him. I can't stress enough how important it is for Christians to get in the Word, to read their Bible regularly, study it, know it. It is your road map to success, and an abundant, fruitful life. It will prevent you from being deceived. Satan always comes to a Christian "sounding like God," otherwise no one would be deceived. Learn to hear the voice of God, and rightly divide His Word.

"My sheep hear My voice, and I know them, and they follow Me." (John 10:27 NKJV)

At first I was very excited and glad to meet my mother, but after a few years and getting to know her better, I finally had to face the fact that we had no common ground of communication.

NEAR DEATH EXPERIENCE FOR KATHY

"The Lord is my rock and my fortress and my deliverer; My God, my strength, in whom I will trust; my shield and the horn of my salvation, my stronghold."
Psalm 18:2 NKJV

On another occasion, while going to Word Chapel, in one of the evening services, Brother Mendenhall stood up in the congregation and asked everyone to begin to pray for Kathy. He had just seen a dark cloud over her. In times past, this cloud had represented death, but it was given as a warning, which, by praying, we could change the outcome. The congregation, as one voice, began to entreat God for Kathy's safety and deliverance. Then Brother Mendenhall spoke again and said "Everything's alright. The cloud has lifted. She may go through something, but it will not be to her death."

The next day while at work, I got a call about noon from the hospital that I needed to get there right away, my daughter, Kathy, had been brought in and was in critical condition.

Kathy was 12 years old at this time, and during the day my neighbor was in charge of them. They had all gone swimming, since it was summer, and they were out of school. Kathy loved the water. All of my children had swimming lessons and were good swimmers. Even though she had epileptic seizures occasionally, she had never had one in the water before. In fact, it usually was very refreshing and would many times revive her and bring her out of the seizure faster, so I didn't worry about her going in to the pool. A little boy had seen her at the bottom of the pool and went up to the lifeguard, telling him that a little girl was on the bottom of the pool. When the fire department got there she was not breathing, but they were able to revive her and transported her to the hospital. When I got to the hospital, the doctor told me that Kathy had nearly drowned, and was still fighting for her life. He didn't know if she was going to make it. Remembering the night before, *I knew she would be okay.* He continued to say that she had so much water in her lungs that many people had died with much less. *I still knew she would be okay.* He continued to tell me that if she did live, she would surely have pneumonia and it would be weeks and maybe months before she would be well enough to go home. *I knew it wasn't true.* He continued to tell me that, if we had made any summer vacation plans, that we should cancel them. *I knew we wouldn't have to.*

They took me in to see Kathy and there were people all around her working with her. Very shortly, she started to go into a massive convulsion. They didn't know she was epileptic and before I could say anything, they rushed me out of the room and I knew they thought she was dying. *I knew she was okay.*

After a while, they let me go back in and the doctor came in to talk with me again, giving me his "bad news" prognosis. Later, when she was much calmer and more stable, he admonished me again not get my hopes up, that she had a long battle ahead. *I knew it was not true.*

I think they all thought I couldn't accept the fact of how serious this was, because I wasn't reacting the way they thought I should. I wasn't crying, fearful, or even greatly alarmed. *I knew she was okay.*

The next day, when I went in to visit her, the doctor said to me. "You might as well take her home, we can't find anything wrong with her. All her vitals are normal and there is no water in her lungs. We are amazed." *I was not!*

REFLECTION

God is so faithful. I believe everyone has a God ordained time on earth. The devil comes to kill, steal, and destroy and he would kill all of God's people if he could. I believe some people may die before God's time, due to various situations; however, Jesus said that He came to bring life and "more abundant life." As Christians, we must stay committed to Him, and pray daily for His protection against the enemy that we might fulfill all of our ordained days, and complete the work that He has planned for each of us.

> *"The thief does not come except to steal, and to kill, and to destroy. I have come that they may have life, and that they may have it more abundantly."* (John 10:10 NKJV)

> *"For you created my inmost being; you knit me together in my mother's womb. I praise you because I am fearfully and wonderfully made;*

your works are wonderful, I know that full well. My frame was not hidden from you when I was made in the secret place. When I was woven together in the depths of the earth, your eyes saw my unformed body. All the days ordained for me were written in your book before one of them came to be." (Psalm 139:13-16 NIV)

I often wonder what would have happened if we had not prayed for Kathy that night when the minister had seen that dark cloud over Kathy. After Brother Mendenhall said she would not die, I believed it as a message from God. When the doctors kept telling me how bad she was, and that she might not make it, I remembered what God said, and it gave me the faith to believe that she would be alright.

"For we walk by faith, not by sight."
(2 Corinthians 5:7 NKJV)

We have to believe the Word of God when we hear it, trust Him, and hold on to the Word no matter what the circumstances, or what the "bad news" voices are saying; keeping our eyes focused on the Word, and putting our trust in Him against all odds.

GOD'S ANGELS STILL AT WORK

ॐ

"Yea, though I walk through the valley
of the shadow of death, I will fear no evil:
for thou art with me;"
Psalm 23:4a KJV

We had not canceled our vacation and all was well for the remainder of the summer, except for one isolated incident with Kathy. Our vacation was a trip back to see Bill's folks in Missouri. We had not been back there since I left in such a hurry several years before. It was time to restore relationships, and we all enjoyed the trip so much.

This time we had a little money and were able to see some of the sights that we couldn't see while living there. Near Branson, Missouri, long before it became a tourist area, we went through Marvel Cave and saw all the sights in the area. They had a train ride that we went on, where bandits representing Jesse James and his gang, held up the train and did a lot of shooting. There were also a lot of log cabins, furnished with replicas of furnishings that showed much of the way people lived in the days of Jesse James. One cabin was supposedly the one that Jesse himself had lived in, including his own bed.

There is a lot of history in that part of the country, and it was all very fascinating to see.

On the day before we were to leave to come home, Kathy wandered off and everyone in the community began looking for her. She had been gone from early morning and it was getting late in the afternoon. In two or three hours it would be dark and it would be hard to continue the search, so a rescue team with planes began searching from the sky as well.

Finally, one of them spotted her walking through a field not too far away. The farmer that owned the field said he had a very dangerous bull in that field. There were signs posted everywhere to stay out. The concern for her safety grew, and there was also a concern about how they were going to get her without being attacked by the bull. Finally, she got close to a fence line and the rescuers were able to get her out safely. The bull was in sight, but he totally ignored Kathy all the time she walked through the field. She had never realized the danger she may have been in. She had left, because she heard us talking about going home the next day and she "didn't want to leave yet."

REFLECTION

Everyone realized that Kathy didn't think like most of us, and we were all very thankful she had been found before dark and was okay. I remembered the time God told me that His angels would be watching over her throughout her life when I could not. Through such experiences I learned to trust God more and more. I thought about the time Daniel was in the lion's den, and an angel closed the lion's mouth.

According to Psalm 34, verse 7, we all have the protection of angels surrounding us. We just have to call on Jesus when we're in trouble. In Kathy's case, others were calling on Jesus on her behalf. She had no idea of the dangers surrounding her.

"The angel of the Lord encamps all around those who fear Him, and delivers them. (Psalm 34:7 NKJV)

UNFORGIVENESS AND BITTERNESS

"Pursue peace with all people, and holiness, without which no one will see the Lord: looking carefully lest anyone fall short of the grace of God; lest any root of bitterness springing up cause trouble, and by this many become defiled;"
Hebrews 12:14-15 NKJV

Another lesson I learned while going to Word Chapel was about unforgiveness and bitterness. I had attended a women's meeting and we were discussing the design of the cover on a song book we wanted to make. I made a suggestion and one of the women strongly opposed my suggestion. I was not prepared for what happened next; for some reason she began to say things to me in a very harsh manner, with words that didn't even make sense. It seemed so unnecessary and out of character for her.

I went home and couldn't get it out of my mind. The next morning, I was doing the laundry, and while hanging out clothes, I began to talk to the Lord about it, and said things like "Lord, she is a much more mature Christian than I am. How could she talk to me like that? It was totally unfair." I went on and on. Finally the Lord spoke

105

to me very strongly, in a very clear voice with one word – "Repent." Then he gave me the scripture about a root of bitterness (Hebrews 12:15). Suddenly, I knew I was allowing bitterness to consume me.

I ran in the house, knelt at my bedside and began to cry and ask God to forgive me. Then a strange thing happened. The Lord showed me this person when she was a little child; how she was verbally abused terribly, by her mother. She was always humiliated, told she was worthless and could do nothing right. She grew up feeling very unworthy, insecure and extremely timid. I began to pray for her, asking God to help me in some way to show her how much I loved her and respected her. My whole attitude was changed when I knew what she had gone through.

REFLECTION

I learned that so many times when people, especially Christians, do something that seems very irrational, hurtful, or just "in the flesh," we need not to allow ourselves to be offended, but pray for that person. We don't know what they may have been through before they came to Christ. Most of us have walked different paths before coming to Christ, some of us have had longer journeys than others, some of us harder journeys than others. We have to be careful not to become bitter and unforgiving when wrong things are done or said by others. If they are Christians, the same God that speaks to you can speak to them. If they're not Christians, we need to forgive them anyway, realizing they don't know what they are saying or doing.

"and forgive us our sins, as we have forgiven those who sin against us." (Matthew 6:12 NLT)

All of us have sinned against someone or against God at some time in our life. If we don't forgive, we will not be forgiven. I am so glad God forgives us all when we ask, and forgets it forever.

Forgiveness is like untying a boat from a dock and letting it float downstream. Let it go. Don't ever look for it again. Unlike God, we may remember the incident, but we need to put it under the blood of Jesus, and never retrieve it again.

Left:
Barbara starting
kindergarten

Right:
Barbara graduating
kindergarten - 1968

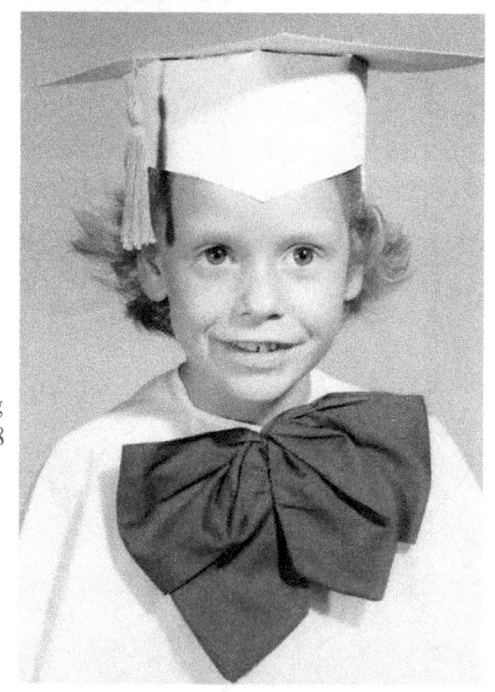

WORKING BARBARA'S WAY
THROUGH KINDERGARTEN

လ∾ૡ

"Foolishness is bound in the heart of a child; but the rod of correction shall drive it far from him."
Proverbs 22:15 KJV

When my youngest daughter, Barbara, started kindergarten, Arizona had no free kindergarten at that time, so parents had to pay tuition if they wanted them to go. The school I enrolled her in was a church school that had grades through the eighth grade. I got a job driving the school bus, in order to pay for her tuition. After the school year was over, they asked me to stay on and help map the routes for all the buses, since I knew the streets in Phoenix so well.

I also taught girl's physical education in the afternoon until school was out, then I drove one of the buses for the higher grades, taking the children home. I will always respect school bus drivers. No one knows how difficult it is to maintain order with junior-high school kids.

The school I worked for was a church school and they had very strict disciplinary rules. The kids could be kicked off the bus if they got too disorderly, and their parents would be called to come pick them up, and most of them knew that would lead to greater disciplinary action.

Once, just as I was beginning to pull out from the school parking lot, the students were so unruly, I couldn't get them to quiet down or even hear me when trying to speak to them. I felt it was too dangerous to pull out on the main road. I stopped the bus in the driveway, turned off the engine, announced that I just quit, and got off the bus. I went to the principal's office and told him the circumstances.

When we got back to the bus you could hear a pin drop. They were all begging me to please take them home, that they would behave. There was one boy that was the oldest of seven children in his family. He was the greatest instigator of disorder than anyone, so I put him in charge of keeping order on the bus. The alternative was that I would quit wherever we were, and call his parents and everyone else's to come get them. I had no problems the rest of the year. I can't even imagine what bus drivers go through today, or that there aren't more traffic accidents.

REFLECTION

The wisdom that God gave me, to bring about order on the bus, was straight from God above. I was ready to quit before God quickened to me what to do. The boy that created so much chaos on the bus respected his father and "the rod of correction," more than the desire to act foolishly.

I'm sure teachers and bus drivers have a special calling to do what they do. After my second year, I felt I just wasn't cut out for that kind of work.

"GOD LEADS HIS DEAR CHILDREN ALONG"

"There hath no temptation taken you but such as is common to man: but God is faithful, who will not suffer you to be tempted above that ye are able; but will with the temptation also make a way to escape, that ye may be able to bear it."
1 Corinthians 10:13 KJV

When Kathy was in the seventh and eighth grades, another thing happened that I am so thankful for. During the time we lived near Glendale, Loritha, my niece who still lived in Missouri, came out to stay with us. Kathy had a lot of problems in school, with kids making fun of her, especially when she had seizures. Loritha was very bright, cute and popular in school. She and Kathy were just three months apart in age and were in the same grade. Loritha stood up for Kathy and made the other kids leave her alone. I didn't even know what had been going on until Loritha told me. Kathy would never complain about anything. It was also during the time that Kathy came into womanhood. Loritha helped her to understand what it was and how to take care of

111

Kathy
8th grade

Billy
9th grade

Loritha
8th grade

Lynn - 5th grade

Barbara - 1st grade

herself. It seems that kids can talk to other kids, even when they're handicapped, getting through to them in a way that adults can't.

I used to worry a lot about Kathy and how she could handle life's different situations when Loritha had to go back home and I wasn't around. There was a lot of talk, at the time, about wars and natural disasters, similar as people talk today. Someone had prophesied that Roosevelt dam had a crack in it and it was only a matter of time when it would break and all of Phoenix would be flooded. I was praying and asking God about what would happen to Kathy, if something like this or other emergencies might happen, and we got separated. She would not know what to do, and my heart was very troubled at that thought.

While I was praying, God gave me the words to a song, "God Leads His Dear Children Along." The specific words of the song that He gave me were *"some through the fire, some through the flood, some through great trials, but all through the blood..."* We don't all go through the same things in life. Kathy would only go through what God would allow, and He would always be with her. Once again, I was reminded that God's angels are all around her and around all those that fear Him. God also brought to my mind the Scripture about how He would not allow us to be tempted beyond what we are able.

"No temptation has overtaken you except such as is common to man; but God is faithful, who will not allow you to be tempted beyond what you are able, but with the temptation will also make the way of escape, that you may be able to bear it." (1 Corinthians 10:13-14 NKJV)

REFLECTION

All people will go through troubles and tribulations in their life. Some go through the fire, others through the flood, others through great trials, but nothing that we cannot bear. We all have a different level of understanding God's Word, and life itself. It depends on the guidance of the Holy Spirit.

Whatever trials God allows to come our way, he has made a way of escape that each Christian can understand. This gave me great comfort, and I have never worried about such things again.

MY HIDING PLACE

"You are my hiding place and my
shield; I hope in Your word."
Psalm 119:114 NKJV

I had gotten a job at a small print shop as a composition person. The job entailed typesetting, manual layout, design, and paste-up. Everything was done manually in those days.

During the time I worked there, I had to contend with one of the most evil men I have ever known. He used horribly obscene language, yelled at his pressman and the other employees continually. For some reason he never yelled at me. I tried to ignore him if he wasn't talking to me; I remained quiet, and did my work without incident. He tried to talk to me on a few occasions, and I just tried to answer with as few words as possible.

He seemed to sense that I was a Christian, so tried to intimidate me, at times, concerning Christian beliefs that he assumed I had. There were times when he began to talk about what he believed, how he had the power to make people do anything he wanted. He said that judges had ruled it was okay for people to do anything

115

that "felt" good to them, they didn't have to obey moral laws, and on and on and on. When I told him what I believed, he got angry and walked away quickly, and didn't talk to me anymore for a long time.

He would then take his anger out on everyone else. He fired his pressman one day – he asked me what I thought, and I told him I didn't think it was very smart, because he now didn't have anyone to finish the job; he got angry again. He hired someone else in a day or two, and belittled him as well, swearing and cursing with every breath. Everything he did was hateful and contemptible; he was a very miserable man. I didn't like working there, but I needed the job and didn't feel released by God to quit yet. Every day on my way home from work, I would stop by our little church and go up to the altar and pray before going home. It was just two blocks from our house.

Once, while I was praying, the Lord showed me a vision of myself as a little girl, all huddled up with my arms around my folded legs. I was under a cleft-like ledge in a little carved out area where I felt very safe. I was sitting there feeling comfortable and safe, when suddenly I heard footsteps coming down the aisle of the church. I knew the doors were locked and in my spirit I knew it was not someone I knew. Even though my body was still kneeling at the altar and my face was downward, my Spirit man looked up and turned to see who it was. It was a very attractive man in a black suit and red tie. He looked very smart in appearance. He had dark hair and by most people's standards you could say he was strikingly handsome. In spite of his appearance, I could see in his eyes that he was all evil, perhaps Satan himself. When he looked at me he didn't smile, but looked at me with great contempt and piercing eyes. He said "If you ever get out of your hiding place, I've got you." I don't know if it had anything to do with the man I worked for, but somehow I felt his spirit was involved. It was comforting to know that he couldn't touch me as long as I stayed in my hiding place.

The working conditions at that place got worse and worse and after two or three more weeks I felt I had to quit. He wouldn't pay me when he was supposed to, and kept putting it off. He told me to come in on a certain day to pick up my check. Knowing that he might put me off again, I took my husband with me. He changed his attitude when he saw Bill, and paid what he owed me without any further conversation.

REFLECTION

I thought many times about whether that man was the one in the vision that I had seen when in Missouri. The vision was of a beautiful sunset and Saguaro cactus, with this man in the foreground. He appeared as though his soul was in tremendous agony and torment, as though he was crying out from hell itself. At that time I felt I was going to go back to Arizona, and would possibly meet such a man. The man that I worked for certainly fit the description, and I believe his soul was crying out in desperation just as I had seen. I only hope that something I said, at some time or other, made him stop and think, and hopefully made a difference in his life.

I remember that vision in the church so vividly about my hiding place. I have never forgotten those threatening words about getting out of my hiding place. Jesus is my protector and my hiding place – nothing can harm any of us, as long as we stay under His covering.

Satan does not have power over us and he cannot cross the Blood line of Jesus. Our covering is the Blood of Jesus. It is like a shield that cannot be penetrated.

Another scripture that has become one of my morning confessions is:

"You are my hiding place; You shall preserve me from trouble; You shall surround me with songs of deliverance." Selah (Psalm 32:7 NKJV)

ANGELIC UPLIFTING

༄ঌ

*"But thou, O Lord, art a shield for me; my
glory, and the lifter up of mine head."*
Psalm 3:3 KJV

While living near Glendale, Arizona, and going to
Word Chapel church, a woman from our church named
Polly and I became very good friends, when I was going through a very hard trial and fighting a tremendous
spirit of oppression. At this time, I was playing the piano
in church. I was struggling with the music, and fighting depressed emotions. Suddenly, I stood up and raised
my hands and began worshipping God. The depression
and oppression lifted. It was miraculous, because just
seconds before I didn't feel like worshipping.

Polly told me later that she saw two angels standing behind me, and they had lifted me up and raised my
arms. It was so encouraging to know that God sends His
angels just to help lift us up at times when we are down.

*"Surely goodness and mercy shall follow me all
the days of my life: and I will dwell in the house
of the Lord forever."* (Psalm 23:6)

REFLECTION

I don't know how people get through life without God; His grace and mercy is everlasting, and is always with us in times of trouble. Since then, I have learned that I don't have to wait on angelic intervention to fight the spirit of depression and oppression that attacks me from time to time. I can say what David said in Psalm 42:11 *"Why art thou cast down, O my soul? And why art thou disquieted within me? Hope thou in God: for I shall yet praise him, who is the health of my countenance, and my God."* David learned to encourage himself, and I can learn also.

Praise always changes the atmosphere.

SPIRITUAL WARFARE

ော

*"For the weapons of our warfare are not carnal,
but mighty through God to the pulling down
of strong holds;"*
2 Corinthians 10:4 KJV

We had another very traumatic experience concerning Kathy while we were attending Word Chapel. We had all been attending church regularly, and one night Kathy heard a specific message on healing, so she decided she was healed and quit taking her medication. Since Kathy was very responsible at a very young age, doing everything she was told to do, I let her control the taking of her own medication. She could remember when it was time, even better than I could. She had been doing this for several of years without incident, so I never considered that anything would change.

I didn't realize she had stopped taking her medication. She had stopped because she was "believing God for her healing." The medication she was on had severe withdrawal symptoms, one of them was that it would create worse seizures, which could cause more brain damage due to lack of oxygen to the brain.

121

About 2:00 o'clock one afternoon, she began to go into grand-mal seizures that were worse than I had ever seen her (except for the first one she ever had at three months old). My first thought was to call her doctor, and then I saw her turning blue. Something inside of me said "Don't call the doctor, call the church." I didn't have time to get to the phone right away, because I immediately started mouth to mouth resuscitation. I knew she had to have air, and even though I had not been trained in CPR, I began to do what I felt was necessary. I believe the Holy Spirit just gave me the wisdom of what to do.

Finally, when her color looked better, I ran to the phone. In those days we only had one phone in the house. It was on the wall in the kitchen – Kathy was in the living room, but still in sight. I called Betty Pope, the pastor's wife, and asked her to call everyone to pray, and that Kathy needed help. I couldn't explain in detail, because I had to get back to Kathy immediately, since she was turning blue again.

Betty called everyone in the church and they all came to the house and continued to pray. Drexel Pope asked that anyone who didn't believe or was afraid, to leave. Several people left. After two or three hours of continually praying, applying cold, wet towels to her face, and breathing for her, her skin color returned to normal, and she calmed down and got up. She started wandering through the house moaning and groaning, and was very disoriented. The thought came to me that she may have more brain damage and was worse off than ever, but I put that thought aside and said "No, I trust God that all is well."

Finally she quieted down and went to bed. She seemed to be sleeping very soundly and quietly, but I fought off fear all night and wondered how she would be in the morning. The next day she was fine.

REFLECTION

I'm glad the Holy Spirit prompted me to call the Pastor's wife. At that time you couldn't just quickly dial 911 and get emergency help. By the time I found my doctor's phone number, explained to the receptionist what the problem was, waited for a call back from the doctor, and probably would have been told to meet him at the hospital with her, she could have died. She was already blue and needed oxygen and I felt I couldn't leave her long enough for a lengthy phone call.

The only way I could think to get oxygen to her was by breathing air into her. It may have not been the best way, but it worked, and she lived.

Doctors can do many wonderful things, and she may still have come through everything okay, because of God's grace and mercy, but I believe when we are fighting against principalities and powers in high places, it is a time for spiritual warfare. This warfare can only be fought by faith-believing, warring Christians, and members of the body of Christ – the Church. Satan lost once again in his effort to kill her.

When God heals us, it doesn't matter whether we continue to take our medicine or not. He can heal us in spite of our medicine. I always tell people to get their healing confirmed by a doctor before going off their medicine.

LEAVING MY COMFORT ZONE

❧

*"Have not I commanded thee? Be strong and of a
good courage; be not afraid, neither be thou
dismayed: for the Lord thy God is with
thee whithersoever thou goest."*
Joshua 1:9 NKJV

Bill had been working for Kar-Go International at that time. The company wanted to start a branch office in Tucson. This was an opportunity for a promotion, and an increase in pay, so when he was offered the job, he took it.

At first, I was very apprehensive about it because of changing schools. New things were always very traumatic for Kathy and things were going so smoothly where we were. After praying about it, I felt it was the Lord leading us, and that it was the right thing to do, so we began making plans. The excitement of a new adventure began to rise. I placed an ad in the paper to sell my piano, because we were planning to live in a mobile home and there would not be room for it.

A Christian quartet group, that was just beginning, answered our ad immediately. They desperately needed a piano and were prepared to purchase it and take

Barbara at the piano - 3 yrs. old

it with them when they came. They were so excited about it. I never dreamed I would ever see them again; however, a few years later they were invited to our church in Tucson, to sing one Sunday evening. They had been doing quite well and were really prospering. They also still had the piano.

HARD TO GIVE UP

The piano was very hard for me to give up at first, but I was moving on to a different era in my life, and I didn't really have time to play it.

When I first got the piano, I played for hours at a time after getting my housework done. They needed a piano player at church, but I wasn't really naturally talented. I had to work hard at playing it. I took lessons for three years as a child when my Dad was overseas during the war. I remembered how to read music and retaught myself after getting a piano.

I wanted to help out by playing in church but they never sang anything in the key that it was written. I didn't know how to transpose the music and read the notes at the same time. I remember sitting down at the piano and staring at the notes, and thinking there must be some way to do this. So I prayed about it. I asked the Lord to help me figure out how to transpose the written music so I could change the keys and still follow the notes.

I went back to the piano later and looked at everything again. Suddenly, I saw all the notes shift up a line or a space and realized it was a different key. I tried it with several pieces and it all worked. I could shift them to wherever they needed to be, depending on where it needed to start; it remained the perfect key all the way through. When playing, I just read the notes a space or line higher or lower, and was able to keep it straight in my mind. That alone was a special gift from God.

When they sang choruses at church with no

127

written music, I learned to follow Betty, the pastor's wife, who played the accordion. When she changed keys, I could play chords and fill in enough to make it work. The church had a new piano player. That was another miracle, as I was never really that good, but God makes the difference. He can raise up anybody to do anything if they make themselves available, and it's His will and purpose.

SELLING OUR HOUSE

After selling the piano so quickly, we were surprised that our house also sold right away. The people that bought it had five kids, and because we had converted our garage to another bedroom and bath, making it a four bedroom with two baths, it was just what they were looking for. They paid us cash, so there was no waiting or qualifying time. Everything happened in less than a month and we prepared to move to Tucson.

A DREAM OF WHAT WAS AHEAD

Not too long before moving, God gave me a dream one night about Bill that was very troubling. It seemed strange to me at the time, because I hadn't seen the side of Bill that I saw in my dream. Only God knows what's in a man or woman's heart, and in time, it can manifest when tested. In the dream, he was very caught up with pride in his accomplishments, thinking he was extraordinarily important. He didn't care about anyone around him, only his own ambitions. I had never seen him like that before, at least not to the degree as he was in the dream.

MY DREAM OF MYSELF

He also gave me a dream about myself. In the dream I "thought" I woke up. I sat up in the dream and saw a table laden with wonderful delicious looking desserts of pies, cakes, candy, donuts, cream puffs, cookies, pastries and sweets of all kinds, beautifully decorated, colorful, and all so tempting. As I looked at all this wonderful food, I heard a voice that I felt was from God. He said "If you don't give up these things willingly now, later you will be forced to." Then I woke up and realized it was a dream. I could never forget it. It haunted me every day of my life for the next ten years. The more I tried to quit eating those things, the more I wanted them. I had always eaten far too much sugar, and later in life it would take a toll on me to the point of becoming life-threatening.

TUCSON – ANOTHER TRAINING GROUND

We left a lot of furniture and other "stuff" behind when leaving Phoenix. We gave most of it away to friends. I've had no regrets and I have never missed any of it. There just wouldn't be room in our four-bedroom mobile home. I felt God was calling us to a new training ground, as it certainly turned out to be.

After leaving Phoenix, with all of its green grass and trees due to all the irrigation, Tucson looked very dirty and barren in comparison, but we would adjust. We always did adjust, and I was okay with anywhere I went, because I knew God was always with me wherever I was.

We purchased a mobile home and lived in a park on the northwest side of town near Miracle Mile and Flowing Wells roads. I loved the names of those streets. All the shopping areas were on the East side of town, until about a year later when a K-Mart store was built about a half block away from where we lived. That was 1970. We were thrilled because with four kids we were definitely K-Mart shoppers.

On the day we moved there, we were driving down Prince Rd. past a small airport on the north side of the street. Just directly across the street was a small print shop. I said out loud "That's where I'm going to work." Everyone laughed. I said "No, I mean it, that's where I'm going to go to work." I loved printing and graphics. I just knew they needed me.

After the kids had gone to school one day, I went there and applied for a job. The owner, Stewart Criss, Sr., was a friendly man, and commented that he had been talking to the "boys" and decided it would be a good idea to hire someone in the front office, but they needed to discuss it and he would let me know.

Meanwhile, I also put my application in at the University of Arizona in their graphics department. Several days went by and I never heard from either place, and since I always expected things to happen immediately, I began to wonder if I should go back to the print shop and remind him of my availability.

I decided to wait till 3:00 on Tuesday, which was the time when he said he would call me. Tuesday morning, the University called me and said they would like to consider my application, and could I please come in for an interview. I told them I appreciated their consideration, but I had already found another job, and thanked them.

As soon as I hung up, I thought to myself, "What have I done? Maybe they won't call me." I waited till 3:00 and no phone call from the print shop. I waited till 4:00 and no phone call. In fact no phone call the rest of the day.

The next morning, I got up and decided to go see them at the print shop again. When I walked in, Mr. Criss seemed glad to see me, but I could tell he had not talked to anyone or given me anymore thought from the time I walked out the door. I knew by his demeanor that he was feeling guilty about not calling me or doing anything after I had left. He said, "Well, come on in tomorrow morning, and we'll see what you can do."

MONITOR PRINTING

The next morning I was hired. This turned into a permanent full-time job over the next five years.

I am always amazed at how God prepares our path ahead of time for things we don't even know are about to happen. There was a reason I was supposed to work at that print shop. In fact, the owner's wife was also the school nurse at the high school where Kathy and Billy attended.

Kathy's problems always required a lot of special attention and patience from her teachers, principals, and school nurses. She was given very special favor, because of where I worked, and because of the relationship of the school nurse and my employer.

Kathy was very high functioning in some areas, so they decided to try her in regular classes rather than put her in the "special needs" classes; however, because she was much slower in getting things done she needed help. The teachers had to work with Kathy continually to help her catch up her work.

Brain damage effects only parts of the brain and the good part tries hard to make up for the damaged areas. So, even if someone tests "0" in certain area, they may be way above average, almost genius level in other areas. This is the frustrating part of working with people that have problems like Kathy. She was probably her greatest enemy at times. She wanted to be normal like everyone else. She would push herself, stay up too late at night, in order to complete her homework, not get enough sleep, which created stressful situations, which in turn created more seizures.

The seizures are caused from a malfunction of the nervous system. The stress and pressure she experienced caused more seizure activity, and as a result, she would end up in the nurse's office at least two or three times a

131

Ann in front of Monitor Prining, 1973

week. Furthermore, there was no medication that could control the seizures completely.

She would become depressed and run away, because of her frustration with herself and not being able to perform to the "impossible standards" that she put on herself.

It became a serious matter and the police had to be involved many times during the years we lived there, because of her need for her medication. Everyone on the Tucson police force, including the captain, knew our family personally. They didn't know what to do. Punishment didn't do any good – Kathy didn't care what anyone did to her. In fact she enjoyed the attention.

Once, when the police had been out looking for her all day long, they found her sitting in a ditch, watching everyone go by. The police chief came over to our car and asked me if I was going to be able to control her. I said something like, "I'm doing everything I know to do." He turned to Kathy out of desperation and asked her "Do you realize that you took the time of the entire Tucson police force away from pursuing dangerous criminals and tending to other important jobs just to look for you? We are going to have to take you to jail and lock you up, if you continue to do this. What do you think? Can you behave in the future and not do this again?" Kathy simply replied very slowly with a soft voice. "I don't know." He just turned, red faced with anger and exasperation, and walked away. During Kathy's high school years, this type of behavior went on for the next four years, but she did graduate. Miracle of miracles!

I spent all of my waking hours running back and forth from my job to the school nurse or the principal. Between problems with Kathy, and then Billy who began running with the wrong crowd, was arrested once for stealing cigarettes from the local grocery store, I can see the hand of God in giving me that particular job, because I was shown more favor than if I had been working at the University. The whole community wanted to help me and didn't know what to do (nor did I).

Billy also had more problems. He seemed to get in trouble more frequently, ditched school often, which he had never done before we moved, and even though he finally did graduate, we didn't know whether he was going to or not until about five hours before graduation. Life had become more difficult.

REFLECTION

When people have to uproot children from school, their church home, in fact, their entire way of life, it can create major problems in the home life. It certainly did in ours. Problems with the two older children, Billy and Kathy, were the most noticeable at first.

The stability of a church home is so very important in raising children. We had become like a family with all the church members at Word Chapel. When we moved, it was never the same. We never did find a church home where we really fit in quite the same way. Our move really upset our comfort zone. When everything is going well, life is easy, but we learn from new experiences.

Just because things are not going well does not mean God is not in the situation. God is with us wherever we are; leaving our comfort zone sometimes stretches us to see how much we really trust and depend on God. We can only work on the areas in our lives when we know what we need to work on.

Changes are a major issue with Kathy, and when they occur, her behavior shows it. I believe her behavior problems were largely due to the change in our lifestyle, and also changes in her medication. We learned years later that she was allergic to phenobarbital and that is what her new doctor put her on when we first moved to Tucson.

Life really never became easy in all the years we lived in Tucson.

LOVE OTHERS

❦

*"And you shall love the Lord your God
with all your heart, with all your soul, with
all your mind, and with all your strength.
This is the first commandment. And the
second, like it, is this: 'You shall love your
neighbor as yourself.' There is no other
commandment greater than these."*
Mark 12:30-31 NKJV

We soon moved into a four-bedroom house that we bought on Wetmore Rd. just a few blocks from where I worked, so I walked to work occasionally or rode my bicycle.

I'd started going to an Assembly of God church that was close to our home. When we first moved to Tucson, I wanted to serve God, but it seemed that every possible position that looked like it was going to open, closed again before time for me to start. I became frustrated, and one day as I was kneeling at my bedside praying, I asked the Lord what I was supposed to do. I wanted to serve Him, but all the doors kept closing. He said two very simple words to me that changed me forever: "Love others." With those two words he showed me that my focus was in the wrong direction. He showed me at that time, that my primary ministry in life would be to people in the "highways and byways" of life, not necessarily in church. I was basing my spirituality on how much I served in church. He only called us to "love others." I had the cart before the horse. He revealed to me a deeper understanding of what He meant by "loving others." It is not what most of us generally think.

I quit worrying about what I was going to do to serve in the church, even though many positions did open up after that, which I served in. I always tried to be more aware of the people I came in contact with in everyday life, and how I was going to *"serve" them.* Every job I had from that day forward, gave me the opportunity to witness to people, pray for people, and yet I never had to announce to anyone I was a Christian. They just knew I was and came to me often for advice and prayer. I had a whole new perspective of the Christian life.

REFLECTION

When things don't work out the way we want them to in life, it may be time to pray and see if we're where God wants us to be. When we try to force a door to open, sometimes we wish we had left it alone, and let God open the door.

When God first told me to love others, I really didn't know much about how to love others, as I had not experienced a lot in my own life; however, I began to pursue it with what knowledge I had.

This command is so simple that many people don't really think much about the depth of it. Do we really love our neighbor as ourselves?

When you truly love others, you go out of your way

to help them when they are in need. You don't just say "God bless you," and walk away. When we really love others, compassion comes into the situation and we will do what we can to help them; doing for them what we would want done for us under the same circumstances. Many of the people we are to love, are not in church. Many people are dying and going to hell every day because someone isn't loving them enough to witness to them, to get to know them, and tell them about Jesus, the only One with real answers that work.

Through the years, I meditated on this a lot, and continued to try to be more outgoing and kind to people. Little by little, God began to change me and show me more clearly what "loving others" really meant. I heard it expressed by one minister that the true meaning of "loving others," is trying to help that other person to become the best he or she can be in fulfilling their dreams and purpose in life. When I thought on this, I thought about how we say "I love You, God." Then I thought, how can we help God become better than what He already is. He's already more than 100 percent. He spoke to my spirit as I was meditating on this and said *"Inasmuch as you do it to the least of these, you do it unto me."* We show our love for God by loving others.

There's no greater joy than knowing you're where you're supposed to be in life and doing what you're supposed to be doing.

LIFE AND CHANGE IN TUCSON CONTINUES

ॐ

*"Unless thy law had been my delight, I should
then have perished in mine affliction."*
Psalm 119:92 NKJV

I had no close Christian friends in Tucson, no one to pray with or talk to, as I had in Phoenix. I felt alone as problems seemed to increase from every direction.

Bill had become a Mason and joined the Shriners. He had a full-dress Harley Davidson motorcycle and lived above all of us in his own kind of way. After becoming a Shriner, and a business manager, he was feeling very important, like he had finally arrived at his appointed destination in life. I never knew where he was, or who he was anymore. The dream I had of him, before moving, was becoming a reality.

He bought a boat, and even though we took a few weekend trips to the lake and worked hard at appearing to be a happy family, we had many problems brewing, inwardly.

GREATER PROBLEMS WITH KATHY

Kathy continued to do things that caused turmoil in the home. Bill resented her and sometimes I often wondered if he actually hated her. Even our doctor told us that we were allowing her to control our family. If we went against her wishes, she made us all pay for it one way or another.

One time, when we planned a trip to the lake, Kathy didn't want to go. We decided that she was not going to get her way and we went anyway, taking her with us. We were at Roosevelt Lake, and on the first morning, soon after getting up, we realized she was gone and we all began looking for her. There were many other people there and everyone began searching for her, as well as, notifying the authorities. The situation could result in a greater possibility of danger to herself because of her seizure activity, and the danger of going without her medication too long, Everyone searched all day. Finally, when someone was coming in to the lake toward late in the afternoon, they saw Kathy walking toward the dam. She was almost there, about six miles from where we were. She was badly sunburned; her lips were burned and swollen for several days afterwards, but it didn't seem to bother her. We all had to leave and go home. We didn't even get our boat in the water. She had won once again.

On another occasion when she did something similar, with everyone showing so much concern and relief over her being found, I happen to glance her direction. She was smiling and appeared to be very pleased with all the attention.

We went to counseling and her doctor on a regular basis. Every time I brought up anything that Kathy did that seemed abnormal, they questioned her. But Kathy could be so sweet and passive that no one considered that she had any dangerous potential. The scratches and

140

scars on my arms and face didn't seem to alarm them. They felt I must have antagonized her somehow to cause the conflict; otherwise, I was doing a great job in working with her – "Just keep up the good work," they would say. No one believed how devious and controlling she could be.

Our neighborhood also began to become alarmed over Kathy. For example, she loved to do yard work, and worked in our yard. Once when she was finished working in our yard, she decided to walk around the neighborhood and cut other neighbor's weeds in front of their house. Because she was carrying grass clippers, neighbors didn't understand that her intentions were not to hurt anyone – she just wanted to clip grass.

Not understanding her, they began to think she was a potential danger to their children and drew up a petition with over 200 names on it to try to force us to move from the neighborhood.

KATHY'S HEALTH ISSUES

At about this same time, we began to notice that Kathy had trouble water skiing and couldn't get back up on the skis. She also fell a couple of times when getting up from the couch to walk. Her knees would just buckle. I told her doctor about the problem. Since he was the head neurologist at the Tucson Medical Hospital, he decided to admit Kathy to the hospital and make her a case study.

Hoping to arrive at a more accurate diagnosis of her problems, his entire team worked with her, running extensive tests, and controlling her diet. She was in the hospital for about five days.

A couple of weeks after she came home, the day before Christmas, he called me at work. I remember it so well, because he was apologetic for calling me with such bad news just before Christmas. His final diagnosis was "a type of muscular dystrophy." He said there was no cure for her problem and that she wouldn't live past 30 years of age. It was very likely it would be much sooner. At this writing she is 59 years old.

[Note: We found out about 20 years later that the doctor made an incorrect diagnosis at the time. The muscle problem was actually caused by the drug Dilantin that she had been taking since she was 3 years old for her seizures. The research discovered that long-term use of Dilantin, after 20 years, caused such muscular problems.]

DEPARTMENT OF ECONOMIC SECURITY (DES)

By this time, DES was involved in Kathy's life and they had recommended that we send her to a vocational school to help her learn to become more independent. She had to learn to ride the bus to the school, and the plan was that I would ride with her showing her every detail of what to do so she could do it on her own.

I rode with her several times, pointing out things on the street corner so she knew she was in the right spot to wait for the bus, having her hold on to the hand-rail getting on the bus, then getting off at the right spot. The bus driver also knew of her condition and promised he would watch out for her.

Things went along well for several days, then one day the people from the school called and asked why Kathy had not shown up that day. I was alarmed; realizing it was already 3:30 and Kathy had left early that morning. I immediately sprang into action, not allowing fear to overwhelm me. We checked with the bus company and found the driver of the bus she had been on. There was a substitute driver that day who didn't know about Kathy's situation and he didn't stop where Kathy was supposed to get off. Since he didn't stop, Kathy just stayed on the bus. He drove to the end of the route which was at a shopping mall, a long way across town from where Kathy was supposed to get off.

It was the end of the line, and the driver told everyone they had to get off, so Kathy got off, not knowing where she was or what to do. She began to walk all day, and finally sat down on a grassy area to rest and took her shoes off. She had some very bad blisters from walking all day. Some college students happened to drive by in a little jeep, and thought something was wrong, so they asked her if she was okay and needed some help. After a few minutes, they realized she had mental problems and was lost.

One thing I stressed with Kathy was the location of the school, where she was going. She told them the address and they took her there. By this time, it was 4:30 and the school was closed, but there was still someone there who knew Kathy.

It seems that the substitute bus driver did not realize that Kathy had to get off at her stop; therefore, when no one was there to get on the bus, he kept going. Of course, he asked us, why didn't she pull the cord to buzz that she wanted to get off. We missed telling her to do that since the regular driver always stopped for her. Once again, God's angels watched over her and He sent a couple of caring college students to help her. When I think back on it, I realize those students could very well have been two angels, because no one was ever able to find them again.

EFFECTS ON THE FAMILY

With what was going on with Kathy, as well as other family problems, Bill withdrew from the family even more. We put the boat and camper up for sale. My other children suffered from not enough attention, and it began to show in many ways. Bill was never around when there

143

Barbara, Lynn, Kathy, and Bill in Tucson - 1973

Randy and Lynn with children, Adam and Angie

were problems; when I would mention something to him, he just told me to "do something about it." I had run out ideas of what to do. We could never discuss anything concerning the children. It was always my responsibility. I desperately needed help.

LYNN AND RANDY

Lynn was always quiet and made good grades in school. She never argued with me or "caused waves," so she probably got neglected most of all.

When she was in the 8th grade, Lynn became involved with an older boy. She was 14 and he was 21, but she was determined to marry him. She ran away with him once, was picked up, and spent a week in the juvenile detention center. Randy, her boyfriend, was arrested and then released because he pointed out to them that they hadn't read him his rights. After much family turmoil and her determination to be with him, the judge consented to her marriage at the age of 15, with the stipulation that her husband be her legal guardian. We all made the best of it and she was married at home in our backyard. There were quite a few friends there, including our friends Betty and Drexel Pope, along with Ray Skelton, another elder, from our previous church in Phoenix. Our friend, Ray Skelton performed the ceremony.

MY FATHER AND HIS BATTLE WITH CANCER

At about that same time in our lives, my Dad became very ill; diagnosed with bladder cancer. Since he was a veteran, he was moved to the Tucson VA to have surgery. Before the surgery, he was able to come to the house for dinner and it would be the last dinner we ever had together.

From the start, he began to tell us what he wanted to do with certain personal possessions like his pickup truck and other things. He didn't believe he would survive the surgery or ever go home again. I scolded him for talking that way and tried to reassure him that everything would go well.

They did the surgery at the University of Arizona Medical Center. He seemed to come around fairly well for a couple of days, then something happened. We believe he had a stroke, even though the hospital didn't confirm it. He was disoriented and not himself. Marguerite, my step-mother, and I went out to see him every morning before going to work and every evening after work.

It just happened that I had an appointment myself for a 6-month health checkup. I had been gaining weight quickly and couldn't even bend over to tie my shoe laces. I assumed it was because I was getting older and that's the way life was. I was in no pain. The doctor said I had a large cystic tumor, about 8" in diameter and it was growing very rapidly. If it burst I could be in serious trouble, so I needed to have it removed right away. My dad was not improving, he also had another more serious stroke and was in intensive care.

I remember going in to see him, as I was concerned about his spiritual condition and wanted to talk to him about it. At an earlier time, he had told me about the time God delivered him from alcohol, so he began going to church for a while, but Marguerite didn't want him to continue, because they "were always asking for money." I knew my Dad had a real experience with God, but in the last several years they had not been attending church. I wanted to ask him if he was saved, but he couldn't communicate very well, I wasn't sure he could understand me either. He must have seen the concern on my face because he said very clearly to me the last time I saw him, "Anna, everything is alright." I felt he was telling me not to worry about him, because he knew he was going to die, but all was well with his soul and he was not afraid.

I talked with his doctor who assured me that he was getting better since his heart was strong. He suggested I go ahead with my surgery, that everything would be okay. He died while I was in surgery.

I had a hard time accepting the news of his death. Bill didn't want to tell me, since I was still in recovery from my surgery. When I kept questioning him as to why Marguerite went home, and who was watching the kids, he finally told me about my father's death. I guess I was in a state of shock and didn't say much, but after Bill left I began thinking about it. I realized that I would not be able to go to the funeral or help my step-mother. My emotions went crazy and I began to cry, then I realized my stitches could break open, so I tried not to cry. Suddenly my whole body began to stiffen.

I tried to reach for the buzzer, but was paralyzed and couldn't move. Another woman, my roommate who was recovering from lip surgery, noticed my situation. She was also a nurse; she jumped up, then ran into the hallway for help. I don't remember what happened next, but I think I passed out. When I came to, I remember sitting up with many dark shadows around me, beating on my back, and yelling at me to breath. I took a breath every time they said to breath, but couldn't seem to breathe normally for quite a while. Everything was dark and their voices seemed to be coming through a tunnel from far away. The next thing I remember, I was lying in bed and my legs were freezing cold. I think I had a mild stroke, even though it was never confirmed that I did. I have had neuropathy in my lower legs ever since, plus I also lost a lot of strength in my hands.

Since I wasn't able to go to the funeral or be with my step-mother, I had no closure at my father's death. It didn't seem real. I felt I had to know where he was.

I asked God to somehow let me know. One night I had a dream, in the dream I saw my Dad as a much younger man, the way I remembered him as a kid. He had a big broad smile and was wearing a hat like he wore in his younger years. It was so real to me, that I accepted it as God's way of letting me know that he was with the Lord. He looked so happy; I can still visualize it in my mind.

TROUBLE WITH THE NEWLY WEDS

Lynn and Ralph (Randy as we called him) began having problems soon after they were married. It escalated when he began growing marijuana plants in a little green house he built outside their back door. Lynn confided this to me one day, and took me there to see it for myself, because she didn't know what to do. She knew if he was arrested, she would be also and didn't know how to get out of the situation. She couldn't divorce him due to the fact he was her legal guardian and he refused to let her go.

I told her she should report him first before someone found out about the plants. She was afraid and concerned about what would happen to her children. One day, she called and told me that Randy had given her a divorce. She agreed to give him complete custody of the children in exchange for the divorce. He owned a trailer right next door, where she could live and take care of the kids, thereby still be in touch with them. Things went along well for a little while; it was as if they were still married.

In order to get the kids back permanently, she decided to call CPS and report him and his marijuana business. Instead of them coming out the next day to do a surprise investigation, they called him and told him of the report and that they would be out the next day to investigate. Around 2:00 a.m., he packed up everything, took the kids and left for Texas where his mother and other family lived. By this time Virginia, or "Angie" as we called her, was 5 years old and Adam was 2.

Randy lied to his mother and all the family about what happened, and when Lynn called his mother to try to find him, no one would tell her anything. The kids thought she was dead according to the story Randy told them.

MANAGER OF KAR-CO INTERNATIONAL TUCSON BRANCH

In reflection, when we first moved to Tucson, Bill's company had selected him to run the new office. He was a pilot and could fly the company plane back and forth for meetings. In fact, they let him keep the plane in Tucson, to use when he needed it. He was not part of our lives, most of the time. I never knew when he would be home. He was so involved with his importance of being the manager over a new business, having the company plane at his disposal, and having employees under him, that he began to take advantage of his position.

One day his boss in Phoenix called him. One of the disgruntled employees answered the phone and said "We don't know where he is, probably out joy-riding in his plane." That comment brought his boss and a crew from Phoenix to Tucson within two hours. When they got there, Bill was still not there, and when he came in several hours later, they fired him on the spot. This brought him back to reality. He got a job in Albuquerque, New Mexico, after that.

I thought about the dream I had about Bill when we were in Phoenix, before moving to Tucson. At the time of the dream, I never thought it possible that a person could change so much, but I saw it fulfilled before my eyes.

He worked in Albuquerque over the next two years, making exceptionally good money, receiving extra pay for travel and living accommodations. The only time he gave us any money to live on, was when I gave him receipts for groceries. He would then reimburse me; that, along with my own paycheck, was how I paid all our household and other expenses.

After Billy graduated from school, he had a hard time deciding what he wanted to do with his life. After he and I discussed this, he decided to go back to Missouri to live with his grandparents for a few months. After that, I lost contact with him for a while, then learned that he married Terri Atkinson, and moved to Washington, where she was from. Over the next few years they had three girls: Melissa, Amy, and Jenny. Barbara and Kathy were still at home with me, at this time.

INEVITABLE DIVORCE

Bill would not consider counseling along with me for our failing marriage, and eventually the separation led to a divorce. The financial responsibility, and the stress of maintaining a home and providing for two children, became more difficult every day.

I heard that Bill had taken a job in Granada, in order to make even more money. It seemed that making money had become an obsession with him. Meanwhile, I began to make plans for my family's future. I put our house up for sale and planned to move into a condominium. I never planned to marry again.

I continued working at the print shop. I was a good money manager and able to keep up our house payments, while saving a little on the side. We lived very simply and always had enough.

REFLECTION

Through troubled times, it helps if a person has a mentor, a good church family, or someone to talk to.

I had none of those things in Tucson, but I believe if I had, I may have handled things differently. The counseling sessions that Kathy and I went to never seemed to help. Kathy was always on her good behavior, and I had a hard time relating what I was going through in trying to deal with the problems. Bill didn't want to hear anything at all, so I just prayed and tried to handle things the best way I knew how.

I was a quiet person, never showing signs of hysteria or panic. I soon realized that if you're not crying hysterically or complaining very loudly, people tend to ignore you, and think everything must be okay. Inside I was screaming for help, but no one could hear me. This experience has caused me to become more aware of "quiet" people and to listen to them more carefully. Sometimes these are the ones that "suddenly" do something that seems out of character, and everyone says "What suddenly happened to them?" when they were crying out for help all along.

God seemed to become farther away as I got so caught up with life and raising my children, but I hung on to my faith, knowing there was no one else I could go to for help. Somehow He brought us through it all.

STORMS OF LIFE

❦

*"These things I have spoken unto you, that in
me ye might have peace. In the world ye
shall have tribulation: but be of good cheer;
I have overcome the world."*
John 16:33 KJV

MOVING ON AFTER DIVORCE

During these years, the children and I had been continually attending church. Billy and Kathy had graduated from High School, but life became harder in many other ways.

In spite of the many problems with Kathy, one night at church, when the Spirit of God was moving, Kathy was filled with the baptism of the Holy Spirit. For the first time, I saw real happiness on her face, and she was much easier to get along with for a while. From time to time, she would still have her violent outbursts. Only God could understand her and could know why she flared up like she did. In Kathy's particular case, her reasoning ability was at a zero level, so when she wanted to do something, and she was told "no," for whatever reason, she would try to do it anyway. Trying to explain to her why she couldn't do it, or that it was in her best interests not to do it at that time, was impossible. Then there was the physical battle, and she would lash out at whoever tried to stop her or told her no.

[Note: Kathy was also still on phenobarbital at this time; we would later discover she was allergic to it. It made her toxic, just like a drunk person. This was possibly the reason for much of her violent behavior.]

We started attending a smaller church by this time, and the Pastor, Bill Hansen, had five children of his own. He seemed to be very concerned about the problems I was having with Kathy and wanted to help us. He owned a motel in town, and suggested that Kathy try working for him, learning to clean rooms. He thought it would be a good chance for Kathy to work and make a little money. She loved to clean and was very good at it.

She still had a lot of behavior problems, but most of her anger was directed at me. A lot of people, including myself, felt that Kathy saw me as someone holding her back from doing the things she wanted to do, and resented my authority. We felt this job would get her focused in another direction, and she wouldn't be spending her time all day at home. She did very well for a few days, then, one day she was asked to do something different from her usual pattern. She began showing behavior problems again, physically attacking Pastor Hansen, and others that tried to intervene. It was finally decided that Kathy had a problem with anyone in authority who tried to get her to do something she didn't want to do. She lost her job at the motel.

KATHY'S VIOLENCE ESCALATES

It is not easy to keep from hurting someone who is attacking you as though they want to kill you. I found myself in such a dilemma every time we had a disagreement over something. When Kathy got angry, she was extremely strong. I soon found I could bump her leg behind her knees and she would fall. Then I could sit on her while having one of the other children go get help. Even though she was struggling and clawing at me, as soon as an outsider walked in the room, especially if it was a man, she became like jelly, and here I am sitting on someone that is not even struggling.

Once, before we were married, Bob came in through the back door during one of Kathy's violent attacks, and was there for a while before Kathy or I noticed him. As soon as she saw him, she "melted" to the floor. He understood better what I had tried to explain to him previously about how violent she could become.

Most people had no idea how violent Kathy could be, except for Lynn and Barbara. Not many people ever saw her when she was like that.

DEPRESSION AND OTHER HEALTH PROBLEMS

About this time in my life, I was desperate to hear from God. Stress and depression was taking its toll on me. When I woke up in the morning, I hated having to live through another day; I had lost my joy. I felt like God had forsaken me and didn't love me anymore. I hated my life, and if I hadn't had the Scripture in my heart, and the many miraculous experiences to remember, suicide could have been an option. I knew I could not do that. I didn't know what to do. I just didn't want to live anymore. I was miserable. No one had an answer for me. Everyone just said "keep up the good work."

After having the female surgery when my Dad died, my doctor put me on some hormones, and soon after my surgery my doctor was killed in an automobile accident, so I just kept taking the hormones, not realizing how strong they were or if there was anything else I needed to be doing. I thought I was supposed to take them for the rest of my life. I felt worse and worse. Sometimes I would be driving down the road and suddenly start crying so hard I had to pull over. There was no logical reason for me to be crying.

During the time I was going through so much depression, I began having some strange health problems. I started going to a doctor who a friend had referred me. He told me my problem was my nervous system. He feared I was about to have a nervous breakdown. He had been giving me some medicine for it, but things weren't really changing. I was having problems with my legs, with burnings and cold-hot sensations, also feelings of depression and despair. For some reason, it was affecting me all over, and I began to think I was dying. I remember calling in Barbara and Kathy and telling them I was very sick, and that I might be dying. I even made arrangements concerning them, in case that happened unexpectedly.

A REVELATION DREAM

One night, I had a dream. In my dream I was surrounded by dark figures in a semi-circle around me. They were poking at my legs, sometimes sharp objects, hitting me, just causing discomfort and irritations, nothing really severe, but wearing me down. I knew these were demons and I began to yell at them to stop. The next day, I called my doctor and told him I wanted to cancel my next appointment and was going to quit taking his prescribed medicine. When I realized Satan was trying to kill me, I began to come against him with all that I knew to do at the time.

I prayed and asked God "Do you still love me? I have to know if you still love me. I have to have someone to talk to that can help me. Please send someone my way that will listen to me." Suddenly, one day when I was praying that prayer of needing someone to help me, I heard a voice over the TV that seemed louder than normal. I had been listening to a Christian station, and it was the only part of anything that I heard. He said *"He shall give thee the desires of thine heart."* (Psalm 37:4) It was the preacher on TV. It was as if God himself spoke to me at that moment. The words seemed to leap out and above everything else. The message was so real that I took it as a "living," direct Word from God. I knew it was God's answer. I didn't know what it all meant, but it gave me renewed hope and I knew God heard me.

One Sunday night at church, shortly after that promise, there was a visiting minister from California. I didn't know his name and had never seen him before. When he walked up to the pulpit after being introduced, the first thing he said was: "I have a word for someone here today." He pointed to me, but the building was packed, probably 3,000 people, so I couldn't tell for sure who he was pointing at. He said again, "You, in the green dress, stand up." I was the only one in that vicinity in a green dress and everyone was pointing at me, so I stood up. He simply said. "The Lord told me to tell you that He still loves you." I needed that Word so much. I'm sure to all those around me that it didn't sound like such a profound statement, but to me it was the restoration of my soul. My life turned around in a moment. My joy came back!

PRAISE BRINGS DELIVERANCE

Near that same time, I also had a dream that totally changed me and returned my joy to overflowing. In my dream I was walking through a corridor of rooms. The rooms were all continuous, with a door at both ends and one room just led into another. As I was walking along, I was singing and praising God – "all blessing, honor, glory, and power to God forever." On both sides of the rooms were high shelves, the demons were lined along both sides of the rooms on those shelves. They were yelling and screaming, and throwing darts at me. But I kept looking ahead, toward God, and singing praises. I heard a voice in my dream say to me "Keep your eyes on me, don't look to the left or the right, continue to look straight ahead and praise me, then nothing can harm you." I noticed from the corner of my eyes, the darts were not hitting me, they were dropping to the ground within two or three feet before touching me. It was like an invisible wall was on both sides of me, and the darts were hitting the wall and falling to the ground. Suddenly, I woke up singing out loud and praising God. I praised and thanked God for the message He gave me, and I realize to this day, that sometimes we have to force ourselves to start praising God when we are down; but it works every time. Our Spirits are lifted and Satan has to flee.

REFLECTION

Storms come into our lives from time to time, but I have learned that they are only for a season. If we hold on to the Word of God and our faith, we will get through our storms and valleys and come out on the other side. Life is full of storms and troubles, and mountains and valleys. Jesus told us that we will have tribulation in John 16:33 *"These things I have spoken to you, that in Me you may have peace. In the world you will have tribulation; but be of good cheer, I have overcome the world."* He is always there with us. None of the storms we go through can begin to compare with what He did for us on the cross. Valleys come to an end, some longer than others, but *there is an end!* Don't give up before getting to the other side. Remember, He is in it with you.

"The Lord is my shepherd; I shall not want. He makes me to lie down in green pastures; He leads me beside the still waters. He restores my soul; He leads me in the paths of righteousness for His name's sake. Yea, though I walk <u>through</u> [emphasis added] the valley of the shadow of death, I will fear no evil; for You are with me; Your rod and Your staff, they comfort me. You prepare a table before me in the presence of my enemies; You anoint my head with oil; My cup runs over. Surely goodness and mercy shall follow me all the days of my life; and I will dwell in the house of the Lord forever." (Psalm 23 NKJV)

A NEW SEASON

"To everything there is a season, and a time to every purpose under the heaven: A time to be born, and a time to die; a time to plant, and a time to pluck up that which is planted; a time to kill, and a time to heal; a time to break down, and a time to build up; a time to weep, and a time to laugh; a time to mourn, and a time to dance; a time to cast away stones, and a time to gather stones together; a time to embrace, and a time to refrain from embracing; a time to get, and a time to lose; a time to keep, and a time to cast away; a time to rend, and a time to sew; a time to keep silence, and a time to speak; a time to love, and a time to hate; a time of war, and a time of peace."
Ecclesiastes 3:1-8 KJV

BOB WILSON

I knew I was coming into a new season after my breakthrough from depression. My mind was clearer, my faith was higher, my joy was restored. I felt blessed with renewed hope in the Lord, that all was well with my soul.

Not long after the church service when God told me that He still loved me, I met Bob Wilson. He owned a business right next door to where I was working. The building was a duplex with a back door. He was in the habit of coming in every morning through the back door of the print shop to get coffee, but I never spoke to him. To me, he was just "another phony salesman," for which I had no use. When he spoke to me, I ignored him.

One Saturday, when I happen to go in to work, I heard a truck drive in next door, and when I looked outside to see who it was, it was Bob. He looked very different than how he looked during the week. He was wearing levis, an old shirt, and wearing a cowboy hat; he looked pretty disheveled. Since his appearance was so different than I had seen him during the week, I was curious, so I went outside, and for the first time I initiated the conversation. I found out that he had been up all night chasing down his horse which had run off after getting spooked by the thunder. All of a sudden, I saw him in a whole new light. I said to myself "He's just a 'dang' cowboy!" This began to spark my interest. *[Note: that was just my way of expressing he was just an ordinary guy.]*

I had already categorized him as a typical salesman, and I didn't care for most of them. I worked in the front office of the print shop and did all the purchasing of paper and other printing supplies. Sales people were always coming in, trying to impress me with their jokes, and most of them were not very appropriate, and not really funny. Bob sold printing supplies, so I had falsely put him in this same category.

GETTING ACQUAINTED

We were both bowlers and I helped teach junior bowling on Saturdays, and Bob had seen me there a few times. Both Kathy and Barbara loved to go bowling.

The bowling alley was just two blocks from where we worked.

I used to go bowl a couple of games on my lunch hour and eat lunch in between. One day Bob asked if he could join me, so I said okay.

After a few "bowling dates" during our lunch hour, Bob began to talk to me about my life, whether I would consider going out with him. We played tennis a few times on Saturdays. I found him easy to talk to, so we became good friends. He seemed to have a lot of wisdom and helped me get through some troublesome times. It was Bob that asked a pharmacist about the medication I was taking. The pharmacist said it was the strongest dose of premarin there was and that it was probably too strong for me. He gave me the mildest dose available, and it helped immensely. A couple of years later, I learned from another doctor that I not only didn't need the premarin at all, but that I was allergic to it, and should never take it again. *[The allergic symptoms: extreme depression.]*

Eventually our conversations led to a more serious nature, and he asked me to marry him. I said "absolutely no, never, I've got too many problems to ever bring anyone else into my life," I was thinking about Kathy. As he pressed me more and questioned me about what "problems" I was talking about, I began to tell him about Kathy. I'm sure he just thought it was a "disease" that could be easily treated with medication. No one seemed to understand the mental problems Kathy had, they only thought of her as an epileptic.

Then he said something that I will never forget "Don't you think it's about time you had someone help you." When he said that, my mind went back to the prayer I had prayed, when I asked God for "...someone to help me." I always thought it would be someone I would meet that I could talk to and could help me, but not

163

necessarily a husband. I hesitated a moment and thought "God, is this your answer – I don't want to miss it if this is you?" I told Bob that I had to think about things and pray for direction.

We never went out on a real date, other than meeting at the bowling alley, bowling a couple of games during our lunch hour, and an occasional tennis game. I considered him a friend and someone to talk to. I knew he was divorced, but I never had any romantic feelings toward him, and didn't think he did for me.

COURTSHIP

From the beginning, and even to this day, Bob has always treated me as someone very special. For the first time in my life, I felt like someone genuinely cared about me and wanted to help me.

After a few weeks went by, with him calling me early every morning, dropping a card on the seat of my car, or placing a rose on my desk, when I returned from somewhere, I finally agreed to go to dinner with him. Every time I turned around he was there. He would drive by my house on weekends. When I went shopping he would suddenly appear. He called me every morning when I got up, and every night at 9:00 to say goodnight.

BOB'S FAMILY

On one occasion Bob took me to meet his mother and sister. I was so impressed with his attitude toward them that I realized he wasn't really treating me "extra special," because he treated them the same way. He waited on his mother with such love and devotion. I had never been around a family like that. He had four brothers and two sisters, all older than he. His father passed away when he was a teenager.

Later, after we were married, his mother's health started to fail and she had fallen several times, so the family members took turns spending two days a week with her so someone was always with her around the clock. When it was my turn, it was two of the most enjoyable days I think I ever spent. She talked about when she was young and first met her husband, and about her trip "out west." They were from Illinois, and were married back there. Her husband went ahead of her to Arizona, to get settled and then sent for her. It was a couple of years before Arizona became a state. She and her mother-in-law rode the train out to Arizona, from Illinois, to be with him.

She was a very interesting woman and did a lot of things in her lifetime. In addition to raising seven children, she opened and managed her own antique furniture store, and took the family to church on Sundays. It's said that she was one of the best cooks in the church – everyone loved her "potluck" dishes. Once she ran a drag race with her son, Jimmy, up and down Cherry Street, an infrequently used street behind the football stadium. Her children were her life and no teacher or principal ever disciplined her children without her being right there to see what was going on, and to defend them if necessary.

She was voted "Mother of the Year" back when all the children were young. Bob still has a copy of a big full page write-up about it in the Tucson newspaper. Bob's father served as a member of the House of Representatives for the State of Arizona for two years, and was also the Manager of Steinfeld's furniture department for 42 years. At that time it was one of the largest and well-known department stores in Tucson.

The kids all tell the story about how their mother taught them to count, long before they started school. Their teachers didn't understand when they got to ten, they continued on with *"Jack, Queen, King..."* Bob's mother also loved watching ball games. In fact when she died, which was not very long after we were all spending time with her, she was watching a ball game, and her heart just "blew out," according to the paramedic. She was in a coma for a couple of days and then just quit breathing.

Bob's family was so normal and well-adjusted. They all genuinely cared about one another. According to his sister Mary, Bob was spoiled rotten, but his mother always said "He wasn't spoiled, he just knew what he wanted, and he got it!"

Well, after meeting his mother and family, I had a whole new image of Bob. I thought he was just trying to impress me by being so nice, but I began to realize that he was just being who he was, and I liked what I saw.

One of the things that really caused me to fall in love with Bob was his objective and blunt honesty. He was not afraid to speak the truth, even if it might hurt my feelings. When he gave his opinion about a matter, somehow didn't sound personal, just a statement of fact, he always spoke the truth. Most people try to be careful to not offend, but he never tried to be careful. You knew you would get an honest answer when you asked him a question. I had never run across anyone before, that I trusted more, to tell me the absolute truth.

TYING THE KNOT

When Bob first asked me to marry him, I didn't feel it would work. I felt I had so many problems and didn't want to bother someone else with them. He told me to take all the time I needed, but he was determined to marry me. Once he said "if it takes ten years for me to make up my mind, he could wait." Finally, I said, "Well, I might as well marry you – you're around all the time anyway."

So, we made an appointment with our pastor, Bill Hansen, for counseling. I wanted to be sure that I could marry again, according to the scripture. I didn't want to go against the Word of God. Bob had been going to church with me by this time, so our Pastor knew us both pretty well.

Bob was concerned because I had said I wasn't sure if I could marry again. On the afternoon of our first counseling session, while he was driving and talking to God about the situation, he suddenly heard a voice in his spirit that told him to look up the following scripture.

"But if the unbeliever departs, let him depart; a brother or a sister is not under bondage in such cases. But God has called us to peace."
(1 Corinthians 7:15 NKJV)

Bob was not really into the Word as much as I was, and when he told me that the Lord gave him a scripture, I sort of dismissed it. When we went to counseling that evening, he told the pastor what God had given him, and it was the very scripture Pastor Hansen had prepared to give me. Not long after that, we were married at our pastor's house with his wife and their five children and my two girls present, along with another minister, Jack Hunt.

Jack and his wife, Mary, became very close friends to both of us. Later Bob went on several prison ministry trips with him. It was on one of those trips that Bob had a special encounter with the Lord. After the service one evening, he was lying in his camper before going to sleep and meditating on things that were said. He suddenly saw a bright light on the wall and a voice that said "Only believe." He replied, "I believe." *[Note: that's really all there is to it. All God wants from us is to*

Bob and Ann - 1975

believe Him. Everything else will fall into place from that belief.] After that we attended Bible studies held in Jack and Mary's home for several years before he had a health problem that led to his death shortly before we moved to Dewey.

Before I married Bob we discussed our spiritual beliefs, and one thing he said was "The only thing I can think of that might be a problem in the future, is that you are much more religious than I am." I think he was thinking I was a fanatic or something, but I just simply said. "One thing you need to know right up front is that you will never be number one in my life. Jesus will always be number one." He felt he could live with that.

He proved over the years to be the help I had prayed for. I know I'm not an easy person to live with; I'm very independent, and headstrong at times, but God is not through with me yet. Bob has his way of helping me change, without being judgmental, and I learned to discuss things before acting on my whims. I've also learned to let him know where I am going and when I plan to return; something that was lacking in my first marriage.

EXTENDED FAMILY

Bob has three children, and with my four, we weren't exactly the "Brady Bunch," but it felt like it sometimes. Even though most of the children were grown, Bob's being a little older than mine by a year or two, there was still a lot of adjusting. After a few years, we realized that your children are your children no matter how old they are, and when there is trouble they always call home.

There was a period of time that we thought we would never get a good night's sleep. When the phone rang any time from midnight into the wee hours of the morning, we would say "Which one is it now!" We also learned to

Bob's Three Children: Jim, Robi, and Shari.

Above: Jim - High School Graduation 1971

Left: Jim & Bob 1998

Below: Robi & son Christopher - 1989

Shari - 8th grade

never take sides. One night we waited up nearly all night after Barbara's boyfriend Rick called at 2 a.m., and said he threw all of Barbara's clothes outside and she was on her way out to the house. We had to go outside to the road which was a distance from the house and unlock the gate. We waited and waited – all night. The next morning I called and asked what happened. "Oh, we made up and everything's alright." Meanwhile they got a good night's sleep and we didn't. The others that gave us a few sleepless nights were Jim and Brenda, Lynn, and Shari. My son, Bill and Bob's daughter, Robi, were out of state and at least not giving us any sleepless nights.

DES INTERVENES AGAIN
CONCERNING KATHY

Kathy was still at home – her job at the motel didn't work out, because of her behavioral outbursts. DES requested that I let them place Kathy in a group home, to see if it would help. They felt a different environment might help her. So I said "Sure, I'm open to anything you can do to help us." I really hoped this was a possible solution. In a short time people were calling me and wanting to send her back home. I refused. I said, "You started this, you need to find another home for her."

On one occasion, she became angry with the woman of the home she was in, and began striking at her and the other residents. The woman put her outside until she could control her behavior, so she started hitting on the big plate glass window off the dining room until she broke it. The glass fell cutting her arms. She kept hitting until she got weak from loss of blood and fell to the ground. They had called 911, but the paramedics still got her to the hospital just in time to save her life.

After several other places, and because her behavioral problems actually proved to be possible dangers for other people, as well as herself, Kathy eventually was placed in the State Hospital in Phoenix. My heart broke for her. I hated to see her have to endure the treatment that she went through. When she lashed out at people to hit and scratch them, they tied her in bed. I cringe when I think of what she went through, even to this day, but it taught her that she had to control her behavior, and she did learn. No one that knows her today would ever believe she had ever had such a problem.

I went through a stage of "anxiety attacks," I believe largely from worrying about her and wondering how she was getting along. I would suddenly wake up in the night, jump out of bed, wander through the house groaning, expecting some impending doom, or that something was wrong. One night during such an attack about 2:00 in the morning, Bob got up and called Betty Pope, and just simply said "please talk to Ann." Actually, I did all the talking and Betty just listened for over an hour, but I felt much better. She was always there for me. I try now to be available to others the way she was for me. *God works through people.*

KATHY MISSING FOR SIX MONTHS

After leaving the State hospital, Kathy was placed in several different homes in Phoenix. I made many trips back and forth to visit with her. There are so many sad stories, it would be a book in itself; I just can't begin to tell all of them; however, one stands out above the rest.

While in one of the homes, a Pastor of a local church began visiting some of the people there and noticed Kathy. After striking up a friendship with her, he asked permission to take her out for a visit. Kathy was agreeable, so the people in charge let her go. When we went to see Kathy she was not there – no one knew anything. Kathy had not returned. Kathy was her own legal guardian and the authorities, or local police, would not step in to do anything to help. We had to do our own investigating, and somehow learned where the house, she had been taken to, was located. We also learned that the man was not an ordained minister; he was a self-appointed pastor of a small group of people. When we tried to find Kathy, no one would answer the door and the blinds were pulled down. It was exasperating, because the police wouldn't help.

I thought that when Kathy didn't get her monthly checks, they would take her back to the home. Since I was the payee for Kathy, her checks came to me. It wasn't until six months later that I got a phone call from a hospital in Alabama, asking if I had a daughter named Kathy Passfield. It seems that Kathy had a seizure in the street and was taken to the hospital. They arrested the man that was with her, because he was black. In Alabama, at that time, a blonde-haired, blue-eyed girl and a black man were suspect. They questioned the man that she was with, and with the information they could get from both of them, they were able to put together what had happened. Evidently, the so-called Pastor that had taken Kathy out of the home, had married her to this man she was with, who also had mental problems. He sent them on the bus to Alabama, and told them to go to a certain preacher's tent meeting to get their healing. He, meanwhile, had taken both their glasses away, telling them that God had healed their eyes. Kathy is legally blind without hers, and the other person was almost as bad, but he led Kathy around everywhere holding her hand. The minister that had married them also told Kathy that God had healed her of her seizures, and she didn't need her medicine. The personnel at the hospital contacted the social security office to get information, which finally led them to me. They put them both on a bus to come back to Phoenix.

Kathy's first Christmas at Mark Allen Manor.

Bob and I met them at the bus depot. Kathy was very glad to see me. She never could express herself much but I could see the relief in her eyes.

It was the most pitiful sight I believe I have ever seen. She had a terrible case of acne from putting Vaseline on her face, and was wearing a long sloppy dress. She was very thin, a scarf on her head, and was like a robot with no expression. The young man, that she was with, led her around, because she couldn't see. He didn't talk much and was very noticeably mentally disturbed; I can't even imagine how they survived for nearly six months on their own. I was reminded again of God's promise, long ago, that He would take care of her and give his angels charge over her when I couldn't.

We took them both to our motel to let them rest and clean up. Afterwards, we took them out to eat. The next morning, we went to the local hospital, and told them the story. They put Kathy back on her medicine and kept the young man for evaluation. I'm not sure what became of him. The marriage was not legal. Nothing was registered.

I can't remember exactly how we progressed from there, either the hospital recommended something, or we contacted DES, but somehow we found a home that had a very good reputation of caring for people like Kathy. It was Mark Allen Manor in Phoenix.

MARK ALLEN MANOR

Mark Allen Manor was a large place with facilities for both men and women. They had a very good reputation with strict rules and structure developed to meet the needs of mentally handicapped people. People like Kathy do not think well for themselves nor are they able to make good decisions. The meals at the manor were very nutritious, and cooked without sugar; they sweetened things only with honey. Kathy had very good success, health-wise, while there. Her seizures were not as frequent, because of the good diet. After a year or two, something happened that stunned us all, even the managers of the home.

When I went to pick Kathy up on one occasion to take her to visit with my sister, Kim, in Scottsdale, we both noticed that Kathy had been gradually gaining weight. Kim just suddenly blurted out "Ann, she's pregnant!" And so she was – about 6 months by that time.

She had been seeing a certain man there. Everyone knew they walked to the store together, and had been together a lot during the day. No one ever suspected anything serious was going on between them. The men's and women's living quarters were completely off limits to each other.

They had dreams of getting married, getting their own apartment, going back and forth as out-patients to get their medication. When her pregnancy was discovered, her doctor was very upset that the home hadn't noticed something sooner, when he could have still done an abortion. He said the chance of the baby being normal was nearly impossible. Both parents were on heavy medications which could certainly cause the baby to have some serious problems, even if it lived.

I was praying about what to do. No one would probably want to adopt the child and it was out of the question that the parents could care for it. I was not in a position to take the baby to raise either.

JANICE AND MIKE METZGER

One day a woman by the name of Janice Metzger called me and introduced herself. She worked at Mark Allen Manor. She and her husband had been trying to have a child ever since they were married. She came from a large family of 10 children. All her siblings had married and had children, but she had had five

176

miscarriages. The last one she carried for five months and thought sure it was going to be okay, but then miscarried again. They wanted a child so badly and wanted to know if we would be willing to let them adopt Kathy's baby. They wanted to start the adoption process before the baby was born and would take Kathy to all of her doctor appointments. For me it was an answer to prayer.

Janice continued to say that she knew the baby might be disabled, but they would love it and care for it just as though it was their own, regardless of any problems. Something quickened inside of me when she said that, and I knew in my heart the baby was going to be well and healthy. It was a special "knowing." God just dropped a gift of faith in my heart concerning the well-being of that baby, and I absolutely knew the baby would be okay.

Everything turned out as was planned and little Tiffany came into this world on August 10, 1990. She was 8 lbs. and perfectly normal, mentally and physically. We stayed in touch with Janice for several years and visited many times with them. She sent me pictures off and on until Tiffany turned 13 years of age. At that time they had moved back to the Midwest somewhere.

One day Janice called me and told me that Tiffany was in Phoenix, visiting with her grandmother during the Christmas holidays. I went by to see her and she asked me a lot of questions about Kathy. I answered as well as I could. We took several pictures. She looked remarkably much like Kathy, with long, blond hair, blue eyes and similar facial features. She gave me her email address and later I sent her an email, but never got one in return. I have never heard from her again; however, we did find her on Facebook. She was just married in 2012 and we downloaded one of her photos.

Kathy, at least, knows that she is well and has a picture of her on her wall.

Kathy's daughter:Tiffany - 3 yrs. old

Tiffany - 13 yrs. old   Tiffany - 21 yrs. - 2012

BUILDING A HOUSE

Before we were married, Bob had been looking at some property outside of town on the northwest side, which were 4-acre parcels. He took me out to see them, and wanted to know what I thought about the area. It was wonderful – so peaceful and quiet – much cooler and a little higher elevation than in town. The lot we finally picked, and eventually built a house on, had 23 saguaros on it, besides a lot of other types of cactus as well, including a lot of desert trees and brush. There was a perfect, natural house site, room for corrals and a horse arena. The area was a little higher elevation than everything around it. We knew it was the one we wanted for our house as soon as we saw it.

Our house on Wetmore had sold by this time, we were able to make a down-payment on the property, and began to draw up plans for our house. We purchased a used 8' wide x 35' long mobile home and put it on the property, while we worked on the house. It was a one bedroom and Barbara was still at home. Soon after moving out there, Shari, Bob's youngest daughter, who was about a year older than Barbara, came to live with us also. They were both in junior high and quite a handful. They slept in the bedroom and Bob and I slept on a hide-a-bed in the living room.

The first thing we did on the property was put farm and ranch fencing around it, and built horse corals. We boarded three horses that belonged to a friend which we had permission to ride, and Bob had his horse, Frosty, so we could both ride when we had time.

It was not easy, but in less than a year we built a home and moved in. We worked under a friend's contractor license and followed his advice on how to do things. We had a lot of friends that came out to help us and we did a lot of the work ourselves. I did all the inside painting – three coats of paint everywhere, including the closets.

That "white stuff" on the trees, bushes, cactus, and fence posts is snow. We were in Prescott that weekend where it <u>didn't</u> snow. We got home just in time to get pictures of a little snow left.

Winter of 1988-89

Our home in Tucson on Lambert Ln.

Above: left - shows entrance way from front gate with snow on the tops of fence rails.

I learned to cut and miter baseboards to fit corners, and helped hold up the insulation for Bob to tack in place.

I remember one Sunday morning about 4 a.m. I suddenly woke up and heard thunder in the distance. The roof had the bare plywood on, but had not been dried in yet. We jumped out of bed, got up on the roof and began rolling on the black tarpaper. We finished just in time before it began to rain, a real downpour.

We were both working full-time jobs from 8 a.m. to 5 p.m. for a printing supply company where we were managers. We got up early in the morning and worked on the house a couple of hours before going to work, and then, as soon as we got home, Bob would change clothes and start working, while I quickly fixed us something to eat. We worked as late as possible, until we couldn't see what we were doing.

When I look back on that time in our life, I don't know how we did it. I know God gave us the wisdom and strength to do what needed to be done, and our contractor kept us on track. We had certain timelines to get things done by, and we were locked into an 11% interest rate, if we were finished by their designated date. The rates were going up and as high as 18% at that time.

Occasionally, things got pretty tense between us. I always said afterwards, that any couple that can build a house together, without someone walking out, can live together forever.

I remember when we were finished doing the electrical work, I could see that we really needed another electrical outlet near one of the vanities in the bathroom. I knew I couldn't say anything. One more thing would delay our inspection, and meeting our deadline was crucial. We had no time to change or add anything, no matter how small it was. It was two years later that I got the outlet I needed.

When the inspector came in, it was late in the day, about 5:00 p.m. All of us were so tired of living in the small trailer and the girls were anxiously waiting to hear his report. When he finished checking everything out, he said, "Well, everything looks good. You can move in tonight!" Then he laughed, and said "I've been wanting to do that for a long time. It happened to me when I built a house once."

We were up very late that night moving beds and other things in, so we could sleep in the new house that night. The next morning when we got up, Shari was sitting at the kitchen table. She said "I feel like I went from poor girl to rich girl overnight."

One evening after finishing the house and moving in, we were sitting outside, enjoying the evening breeze. We both agreed that we loved it there so much we would never sell or move no matter what. We would not even take $85,000.00 for it, which was over twice what our original mortgage was at that time. We had no idea that the value of the land and everything would escalate to over three or four times that much in the very near future, or where life would soon take us.

CHANGING JOBS

We quit the supply business, and both of us went to work for another printer in town – Bob worked in outside sales, and I worked in the graphics department. After about six months, I was promoted to customer service and job estimating.

One of the customers there didn't care for the work the new graphic people were turning out, and asked me one day, if I had ever thought about going into business for myself. I really hadn't, but she kept pressing me, and said that "with all the business they had, she was sure their business alone would provide me enough business that would amount to at least as much as I was making at the time, and probably more."

The stress intensified from the company where we were both working, because our employer was facing possible bankruptcy and wanted estimated values on jobs when work came in, which was my job. I had to work with actual costs and "real" numbers and timelines. I couldn't just pull the numbers out of thin air. He put a lot of pressure on me to get him the information quickly. He then took these figures to the bank and borrowed money against them to keep the business going. The stress became too great and I totally collapsed one day, walked out and went home, came back the next day and quit.

REFLECTION

This new season in my life came about so suddenly, it seemed like a miracle. It reminds me that if we continue to trust God, He always has great things in store for us. We must not faint or give up, if we want to come in to the things that God has for us.

> *"And let us not be weary in well doing: for in due season we shall reap, if we faint not."* (Galatians 6:9 KJV)

I would never have believed my life could turn around like it did. Even though we still endured many storms together, Bob seemed to have great wisdom that always amazed me. He knew how to do things I didn't. I am reminded again of the following verses:

> *"Two are better than one; because they have a good reward for their labour. For if they fall, the one will lift up his fellow: but woe to him that is alone when he falleth; for he hath not another to help him up."* (Ecclesiastes 4:9-10 KJV)

I often wonder where I would have been if God had not answered my prayer and intervened in my life. The enemy wants to destroy us, but God gives grace and mercy to the humble. We just have to cry out and call on the Lord in our times of distress.

ANGELIC INTERVENTION

৩৯৫৩

"God is our refuge and strength,
a very present help in trouble."
Psalm 46:1 KJV

While Barbara and Shari were still at home, the three of us were driving down Orange Grove Road one day on our way home. We had a small Volkswagen rabbit (the new model that came out in the middle '80s). Suddenly, a large dog ran out in front of us and I, instinctively, swerved to miss the dog. The car began to fishtail, and even though the road was paved, it was narrow and there was a gravel drop-off from the pavement. I had crossed over to the other side and the car started turning up on two wheels, and was beginning to slide off into the gravel on the opposite side of the road. I was trying hard to hold on to the steering wheel and bring it around, but I wasn't strong enough to stop it from flipping back and forth. I heard Barbara in the background pleading the Blood of Jesus while I was praying "God, help me to hang on to this steering wheel." Suddenly a mighty strong force came over my hands and I felt a supernatural strength as I held on to the steering wheel, and brought the car back over on all four wheels. I was able to get back on the road without an accident. I know in my heart that it was divine intervention that day. It had to be a ministering angel sent from God to help us.

Even the fact that no cars were coming from the opposite direction was a miracle. After we were safe again, Shari said to Barbara "Wow, I didn't know you knew how to pray like that!" We were all pretty shaken up and knew we had experienced a supernatural intervention.

Shortly afterwards, both the girls moved out. Shari went back to California with her mother, and Barbara left home to live with her boyfriend, Rick, to start her own life. She was just 15 and I could not give her my blessings; however, we had an understanding that I would always be there if she needed help, and to call me if she needed me. She was going to go regardless, and I didn't want to destroy all bridges of communication.

REFLECTION

When we're in trouble we just have to call on the Lord. It's possible that if I had not called out for help when our car went out of control, or Barbara had not prayed, we might not be here today. Satan had destined a very serious accident for us that day. He is the destroyer, but God is the life-giver. He came that we might have life and have it more abundantly.

"The thief cometh not, but for to steal, and to kill, and to destroy: I am come that they might have life, and that they might have it more abundantly." (John 10:10 KJV)

It broke my heart when Barbara decided to move out to start her own life at such an early age. I knew she was not prepared for what the world had to offer. Barbara was my youngest and I cried a lot of tears over her.

Many people try to get ahead of God and make moves before they're ready, or just don't ever consider God when they make their plans. I think I know how Jesus must have felt when he grieved over Jerusalem.

"O Jerusalem, Jerusalem, you who kill the prophets and stone those sent to you, how often I have longed to gather your children together, as a hen gathers her chicks under her wings, but you were not willing!" (Luke 13:34 NIV)

So many times, I wanted to draw Barbara close to me, love her, shield her, and just help her get through life in a much easier way than the path she chose, but she "would not." I think God must feel that way today about His creation. So many people going their own way, without a thought or care about their Creator.

Chapter 3

THE LATER YEARS

RUNNING A BUSINESS

☙❧

"But thou shalt remember the Lord thy God:
for it is he that giveth thee power to get wealth"
Deuteronomy 8:18a KJV

Bob and I both had very specific skills which complemented each other. I was strong in typesetting and prepress graphics, and he was strong in the printing business. Through the years, it was because of this that we actually were able to survive when many businesses didn't make it. When one area of work was slow, the other made up the difference, and we soon learned to overlap into each other's fields.

It was 1978 when we became "Sunrise Graphics, Inc." I quit my job, and started doing typesetting and graphics. Bob also quit his job a few months later, and began brokering printing jobs. In the beginning, we had just one customer with lots of work, but things began to grow pretty fast. Throughout the years, our best advertising was "word of mouth."

We started our business in our home, since we had plenty of room after Shari and Barbara moved out. They had shared a large 20x15 ft. room which was ideal for

191

me to use for my graphics business. One of the other bedrooms became our office, our garage became our camera room where we installed a dark room. We added an enclosed porch on the back of our home where we eventually added a printing press.

When we first started, I worked a couple of days a week for another free-lance typesetter, and in exchange for helping her, I was able to use her equipment to do my own work. Within a year, I was able to purchase my own equipment.

GAIL – SURELY AN ANGEL SENT TO HELP US

One of the greatest blessings which happened to us, that really helped launch our business soon after we started, was to hire a girl that we met through a friend. She contributed more to our business getting off to a good start than any other person. Her name was Gail – can't remember the last name. Her husband made enough money without her working; for some reason they had a limit as to how much they could make, so she didn't want any pay, but she was bored and wanted something to do. She was from Georgia, with only a fourth grade education. I originally intended for her to just come in mornings and make copies and put the coffee on, so I could get a few more minutes of sleep, since I was working until very late every night.

The process was that I would type all day, putting the data on large 8" floppy disks. When finishing a job, I would put the disk in the typesetter to print what came out on high-resolution photographic paper. It took forever to print, so at night, I would set things up to run and go to bed. The machine was very loud, and as long as it was running I would sleep; when it quit, I woke up, and changed the disk, then went back to sleep. This went on for months, until I got a second machine and could alternate between the two. The galleys of type would be on the copier when Gail came in the next morning.

When I was typing invoices one day, she asked what I was doing and asked if she could do it, so I could get back to my typesetting. She sat down at that typewriter like a pro. I was very impressed. I didn't even know she could type. She then said she could make copies of the galleys of type, and proof-read for me if I wanted. She was the best proof-reader I ever had. Nothing got by her. She read with the dictionary at her side.

Anything she saw me doing that wasn't "making money" for us, she insisted on doing it so I could work at what she couldn't do. I was amazed at how smart and capable she was with only a fourth grade education. After a few months, she announced she was moving back to Georgia, because she "missed her mama." We offered her 10 percent of our business if she would stay and work for us, but she insisted she had to go. I will never forget her and all that she did for us to help us get our business going.

LINDA WEBER

About that time, Linda Weber came into our life. We needed to borrow some money to purchase another typesetting machine, and the bank needed financial statements and other things that I had not a clue as to what they were talking about. The bank president with the First National Bank in Tucson had gotten acquainted with Linda through some of his other customers. He called her and asked her to go see us and see if she could help us put some information together for him. He really wanted to help us. After Linda got together what he needed, he gave us the loan we needed. He became a close friend for a long time, and so did Linda. In fact, she has become a life-long friend. She is still our personal accountant.

Linda Weber

Left: 1978

Below: 2014

Finally, a business that decided to upgrade their equipment sold us their old typesetting machine and also gave me enough work to help pay for it. It was no time until it was paid off. We purchased another machine and hired our first employee to help us; then another employee, and then several people. We had landed a huge government contract to typeset and produce all the manuals for Davis-Monthan Air Base.

After a couple of years the business outgrew our house, and we decided to move it into town. We rented a small unit on Grant Rd., close to the I-10 freeway. After the first year, we rented the one next to it, and opened up the wall in between.

TIME OUT TO LEARN SQUARE DANCING

In the early years of our business we had a little time to do something other than work. So, after some prompting from friends, we decided to take up square dancing, and that is where we met Nate and Geri Bliss. Nate was a great square dance caller and they were fun to be around. After graduating from the beginner's level of dance, we went with them to a Plus Level workshop in Colorado over a three-day weekend. We came back Plus Level dancers, and continued dancing at least one night a week. It was good exercise and we met a lot of nice people.

OUR ONLY VACATION

We took a 10-day vacation in 1984, which would turn out to be the only vacation during the entire 12 years we were in business. We drove our truck and trailer with our boat on it, and envisioned doing a lot of fishing along the way. We first stopped in California, where we went to a square dance one night, then drove up to Versailles, California, near Reno. Nate Bliss had divorced, remarried and settled down there. He started his own construction remodeling business, but still called square dances a

Ann & Bob - Square Dancing

couple of nights a week and he loved fishing. We stayed there two days and did a lot of fishing and went to a dance one night.

From there we went to Washington to see my son Bill and his family. We rented a little cabin near the ocean. Bill's wife, Terri and their children and I stayed at the cabin and relaxed on the beach while Bill and Bob went deep-sea fishing for salmon. We went through Oregon, and across to Montana and Wyoming, hoping to visit some friends there, but missed them. We came back through New Mexico, and home again. We had a flat tire on the trailer once in Wyoming, but other than that, we didn't have any trouble. We towed that trailer and boat the entire trip and never put it in the water once.

The only other short weekend vacation, was a trip to Yuma where we went to a square-dance convention with our travel trailer. The heat was far worse than Tucson in the summer. At least we had a cooler on our little trailer, and a comfortable place to sleep at night.

When going to our first dance, we realized we were with a completely different class of square dancers than we were used to. They were accustomed to the heat and dressed accordingly. None of the women wore big ruffled petticoats, like the women in Tucson wore; however, they did wear the square dance dresses. Well, we got through the weekend, and felt fortunate that we had a cooled trailer to retreat to, but both of us felt we would never go to Yuma again in the summer to do anything that involved any exertion.

BACK TO BUSINESS

Meanwhile, after moving closer to town, our business began growing at a very rapid pace. Soon we had 10 employees; I wish I could say that everything was always great but it was not!

I learned that people lie on their résumés, they gossip

and complain about each other, and they won't clean up their messes in the kitchen. Some would get to work late or not at all. When someone didn't show up, Bob and I had to take up the slack and worked 16 and sometimes 20 hours a day to meet deadlines and get the work finished. We couldn't afford to pay overtime.

Once, I didn't finish a job until 4:00 a.m. the next morning, so I decided it was not worth the effort to drive home and come back by 8:00 a.m. We lived way out of town, about five miles south of Marana. I just stayed, and worked through the next day.

HEALTH ISSUES BEGIN

The stress of working so many hours a day, eating far too many sweets, especially candy, was beginning to take its toll on me physically. I wasn't getting enough "real" exercise, gained too much weight, and was constantly under stress.

One day, as I was typesetting something that I had been working on, non-stop for about five hours, the phone rang. I kept working, waiting for someone in the office to answer it, but they weren't at their desk, so I jumped up to go answer it. A voice spoke to me so clearly, "Sit back down, or you won't make it across the room alive." I sat back down, took a couple of deep breaths, and let the phone ring. That was a wake-up call for me to make some changes in my life-style. I joined "Naturally Women," a fitness club for women, and began taking water aerobics classes.

I also realized, it was time for me to deal with the problem of eating too many sweets. I remembered once again the dream I had before we moved to Tucson. I had gotten to the place where I couldn't sit down and complete a difficult job, especially forms, or something that required a lot of concentration, without a bag of candy beside me and something in my mouth.

In those days, you could not see what you were doing on your screen, and forms required a lot of special code. You had to keep the picture in your head to know where you were. The candy became essential for me to be able to concentrate. Sometimes, if I ran out of candy, I had to go to the store for more before I could finish what I was working on. This process was also slowly killing me.

By this time, I had had a couple of experiences of passing out. My doctor told me that if I didn't change my way of eating, I could go into a coma and never wake up. I tried everything I could to change, but nothing lasted long. I knew I was killing myself.

Through that experience, I can only imagine the misery and torment that drug and alcoholic addicts go through, when they know they are hooked, and no longer have control.

Finally, one evening when I was alone, while I was sitting at the counter in the kitchen and I began to call again on God for help. I poured my heart out, telling Him I just couldn't quit eating candy on my own, that I needed supernatural help. After a good night's sleep, I got up the next morning, and headed out to work. I never ate breakfast and usually just grabbed a handful of candy to eat on the way. I was almost at work when I realized I hadn't taken any candy with me or even thought about it. I also didn't want any. Oh, praise God! He had set me free. I never touched another piece of candy, or anything sweet, since I knew I couldn't stop with just one. My health was restored as I continued the aerobic classes and eating healthier. I lost weight and had renewed energy.

DELIVERANCE FROM MIGRAINE HEADACHES

Not long after that our friends Jack and Mary Hunt wanted us to go on a camping trip with them in the White Mountains over a weekend.

I had had migraine headaches frequently for years. They started sometime after moving back to Arizona from Missouri, in the middle 1960s. When I try to think of some common denominator that may have contributed to them I believe it could have been the excessive sugar I was eating.

Sometimes when I would have them at work, I would just have to go to my office, lock the door, turn out the light, and lie down on the floor with my pillow until I slept it off. Sometimes it would be most of a day and night before I could function enough to go home. There was no medication that seemed to help.

Well, on our camping trip I developed a migraine on the trip there. As soon as our tent was set up, I had to just lie in bed the entire weekend. I couldn't stand noise, light, or talk to anyone. When everyone was ready to pack up and go home, I sat on a chair outside the tent with my head down, trying to avoid the light and be as still as possible.

Jack happened to walk by me to put something in the car, studdenly he stopped and reached out and prayed for me. He no sooner said "Amen," when I suddenly began to expel fluid from my skin and in every way possible. I threw up and ran to the "outhouse tent," the men had set up. I had diarrhea, and continued to throw up. I was wringing wet with sweat. Afterwards, I was extremely weak, and could hardly walk to the car where they had prepared a place for me to lie down. To this day, I have never had another migraine headache. Whatever was in me that caused the migraines came out violently and forcefully.

[Note: I'm not sure what brought on the migraines to begin with, but sugar is a strong suspect. If I had gone back to eating sugar after being delivered, I may have begun to have migraines again.]

200

UNCONDITIONAL LOVE

That was also about the time that God revealed to me His unconditional love. My father had always been a very strict man, not mean, but "militarily" strict. He ran our household like the military. "Hit the deck!" was our wake-up call in the morning. No one ever slept past 7:00 a.m. in the morning, even on holidays and weekends. A command was given and always followed. We had been taught to obey without question, whatever we were told to do. I never considered whether there might be an option, or whether I knew how to do whatever I'd been asked, we just did it without question, figuring it out as we went. For me, this carried over into our business.

One day, when a customer came in with a job that was a little difficult, it never occurred to me that I had the option of telling them that it was not really our expertise. I had been programmed to do whatever I was asked, so therefore, I would take in the job, struggle with it, spending way too much time, and even though the finished result was satisfactory, I couldn't charge for all the time that was spent on it. One day when such a job came in, while trying to figure an estimate on it, the Lord spoke to my spirit, "You don't have to know how to do everything, and I still love you." He made me realize that I had always felt I had to know how to do anything that anyone asked of me, even if I had not been taught.

My father never considered whether we knew how to do the things he told us; we just had to figure out how to do it, and do it quickly. For the first time, I realized I could say "No, this is not what we specialize in, why don't you take it down the street to another printer. They can give you a better price on it, because it's more their specialty." What a great burden was lifted off my shoulders that day, when I knew that it was okay not to know how to do everything, and God still loved me.

Ann setting type - Bob running the small press

NEW TECHNOLOGY

When we first started our business in 1978, personal computers were almost unheard of. Typesetting machines were very much like some of the early computers, but with many more features in some areas but less in others. They used a floppy disk to load the machine, and other disks to load various fonts. There were no hard drives for storage, but there was a floppy disk to store the computerized type. Everything was done using codes similar to HTML as used in creating web sites.

In the '80s Apple came out with a computer that would "talk" to Mergenthaler typesetting equipment. By this time, many people began to own personal computers, and especially businesses.

We purchased a computer and I took an evening course at Pima College to learn enough to get started with what I needed to know. Some of our businesses wanted to start sending us copy electronically, instead of us doing all of the input as we had in the past.

There was only one problem – getting the raw type into my typesetting machine, so that it could be formatted and printed out on high resolution paper. Computer printers were the biggest obstacle in turning out professional looking copy directly from the computer, in the early years.

We had purchased a Mergenthaler typesetter and we had a computer, but no one locally knew how to get the copy from one machine to the other. The salesman from Mergenthaler told me I would have to contact the manufacturers of both pieces of equipment and get the hexadecimal numbers for every keystroke on each machine. Then I had to create a "basic" batch file, which I had learned how to do in my computer course, to send to the typesetter. The batch file had to tell the typesetter's hexadecimal numbers for each character, to equal the hexadecimal number to the equivalent character in the computer. We then had to connect the two machines with a serial cable to transmit the copy. The batch file would be sent ahead of the computer copy and everything could be read in the typesetter and it worked.

There were so many times, during the next few years, that I just had to pray and ask God to show me what to do concerning computer problems. There was no local support for what we were doing, and we were the first in the area to have such equipment. Many times God would reveal to me around 5:00 a.m. in the morning, just before awakening, what I needed to know. It would come to me like a sudden "idea." It was like a true revelation, and the answer worked 100 percent of the time.

"Thus says the Lord, your Redeemer, The Holy One of Israel: 'I am the Lord your God, Who teaches you to profit, Who leads you by the way you should go.'" (Isaiah 48:17 NKJV)

God teaches us to profit, and leads us by the way we should go. The Holy Spirit is our teacher and guide. When we listen to Him we always profit from it. He was truly our guide in our business and showed us many times which direction to go, and, miraculously, gave me revelations, that helped get us through seemingly impossible situations.

LET THE STRONG UPHOLD THE WEAK

One night, when working late, Kathy called me from the group home she was staying at in Phoenix. She asked me what seemed to be a simple question and I gave her what I thought was a plain, easy-to-understand answer. I had given her a phone card, so she could always call me about anything she needed or was troubling her.

About 15 minutes later she called again, with the same question. Kathy was on a lot of medication for her seizures, and it affected her memory and alertness, so I patiently answered her again. It was late at night and I told her to go to bed and get some sleep, and she could call me the next day, if necessary.

Well, I just got back to working on my project, starting to make good progress when the phone rang again. It was Kathy asking the same question. I answered her again and told her once more to go to bed; however, she continued to call me back several times over the next hour. By this time, it was about 11:00 p.m. at night and I had to finish what I was working on, go home, and still be back to work by 8:00 a.m. in the morning. When I got the last phone call, I answered her question, one more time, and very firmly told her not to call me back that night. It was late, and she needed to get to bed.

After hanging up, I sat down and began to cry. With my head in my hands and feeling exasperated and sorry for myself, I said, "Lord, why do I have to put up with this?" A very soft voice spoke to my spirit and said very clearly, "Would you rather be Kathy?" Along with it the words "let the strong uphold the weak," came to my mind. I thought of the following scriptures.

"We then who are strong ought to bear with the scruples of the weak, and not to please ourselves." (Romans 15:1 NKJV)

"Now we exhort you, brethren, warn those who are unruly, comfort the fainthearted, uphold the weak, be patient with all." (1 Thessalonians 5:14 NKJV)

The essence of the message was that, anytime "we think" we are stronger or more capable than another

205

Ann and
Marguerite

About 1987

Bob and
Marguerite

person, it is our responsibility to help that person in their weaknesses. I realized how fortunate I was not to have a disability, and was strong enough to help another person. I answered the Lord, "No, Lord, I would not rather be Kathy. I will be the strong person." It was like I made a choice that day, and assumed the responsibility that comes with being the strong person. I changed my attitude that night, and to this day, I have not gone back on my decision or ever complained again.

FINANCIAL STRUGGLES

Sooner or later, new businesses begin to have financial issues, especially when there are a lot of employees to pay, taxes, and other regular expenses such as rent and utilities. When economic times started a down-turn, as they did in the middle to late '80s, we began to feel the "crunch," as did many other businesses.

We had a lot at stake concerning our business. We had already borrowed money against our house with a 2nd mortgage. Every penny we made went back into the business; everyone else got paid before we did, in fact, I didn't get paid at all. Bob was the only one that got paid, so he would have enough to eventually draw the maximum Social Security benefits when he retired.

We had no private life, and after the first couple of years, we stopped square dancing, except on the weekends when we went to Prescott, Arizona, to visit Marguerite, my step-mother. We did her yard work, and maintenance and upkeep on her home. There was square dancing at the courthouse square every Saturday night. She always insisted that we go.

We also continued going to church and paying our tithe. We were both very healthy with lots of energy, and I thought we could always make things work by just working a few more hours in the day. After a while,

I realized there were no more hours in the day, and we began to feel like we had a "bull by the tail" and couldn't let go.

We took in any type of job that came along. God had blessed us both with a lot of wisdom and skills. Some of our customers began to call us "Anything-for-a-buck-printers." How true it was!

I always thrived on pressure and hard work, but there came a time when I said "God, help me, I've had enough!" We put the business up for sale and never had anyone come and even look at it. If anyone had come in and just said they would take it over, I would have been willing to walk away and let them have it.

About the mid to late '80s many businesses in the area were closing down, but we had to keep going, because everything we had was tied up with our business. It was either make it or lose everything. So we just "kept on keeping on," an expression my Dad had always used.

VIRGINIA (ANGIE) COMES TO LIVE WITH US

Later, after 7 years, Lynn finally was able to make contact with her children again. I believe it was because Randy was in trouble and couldn't manage them anymore.

When Angie was 13 years of age, she came out to Tucson. She stayed with Lynn for a short while and got in trouble and was arrested. No one really knows all the story of how she was raised during those seven years, but the bits and pieces sound like a horror movie. One day, an officer of the juvenile detention center called Bob and I asking if we could take her in, after Lynn had tried to help her and did all that she knew to do.

After discussing it very thoroughly with the judge, they promised that if she was more than we could handle, they would take her back and place her elsewhere, we agreed to take her. We were working long hours at our business right then, and didn't know if we could handle all the problems of a troubled teenager. It proved to be even worse than we had anticipated.

Angie lived with us for about a year. She went to counseling on a regular basis, attended high school, had a baby, and was the "sweetest" straight-faced liar you would ever want to meet. I loved her dearly, and still do, but just could not reach her or know what to expect next.

The end result of her living with us, was that when she got pregnant, she went back to her mother. Lynn's plan was to keep the baby and help her once again; it didn't work out and the little girl baby was put up for adoption. In another year she was pregnant again, and she went to stay with the couple that wanted to adopt her baby. After Breanna, her second child, was born we had a good relationship with the couple that adopted her and got to see her frequently, until they moved to Sahuarita, Arizona, and we moved to Dewey, Arizona. Every year or so we got an updated picture of her until 2012. She's grown now, a beautiful young woman and looks much like Angie.

Over the years Angie went through some very hard times, but eventually met Rich and has stayed with him. She settled into a beautiful, well-adjusted woman, with God's help and many, many prayers. Her story is too great to tell at this time (it is a book in itself).

MORE BUSINESS PROBLEMS

Well, we really had our hands full with family problems, as well as, trying to grow and run our business.

One day, Bob came to me and said "I think we're going to have to quit tithing for a while, we just can't afford it." It had been very hard, so I told him we would try it for a few weeks. I was uncomfortable with the

Lynn with Adam and Angie when they first came back to Tucson.

decision from the beginning, and it seemed that things just got worse and my conscience bothered me to the point that I had a hard time praying and asking God for help or to bless us, because, according to Malachi, we were robbing God.

"Will a man rob God? Yet you have robbed Me! But you say, 'In what way have we robbed You?' In tithes and offerings. You are cursed with a curse, for you have robbed Me, even this whole nation. Bring all the tithes into the storehouse, that there may be food in My house, and try Me now in this," says the Lord of hosts, "If I will not open for you the windows of heaven and pour out for you such blessing that there will not be room enough to receive it. "And I will rebuke the devourer for your sakes, so that he will not destroy the fruit of your ground, nor shall the vine fail to bear fruit for you in the field," says the Lord of hosts; and all nations will call you blessed, for you will be a delightful land," says the Lord of hosts." (Malachi 3:8-12 NKJV)

I just couldn't live like that, and told Bob we had to go back to paying our tithe if we expected God's blessings on our business and in our lives. He agreed and we went back to tithing.

[Note: Anytime our conscience condemns us about anything, whether the rest of the world agrees or not, it breaks our fellowship with God, and we can't go boldly into the throne room with our petition.]

I started going in to work at about 6:00 a.m. in the morning, before anyone else got there at 8:00 a.m., when we opened. I would go throughout the shop from one department to the next, and pray over the work, and for the people that would be working there that day. I prayed that no mistakes would be made, that things would run smoothly, that there would be no dissension between employees, and that God would show us great favor with each other, with customers and suppliers, basically that all would go well with everyone.

Mistakes can be very costly and we couldn't afford to make any or have to redo any jobs. We had some very good employees at the time, and especially our pressman. He looked over the negatives and plates very closely, before he put them on the press. If there was anything wrong he would spot it. The person that made the plates (which was Barbara at the time) didn't like having to redo them, but I told everyone "Anything he tells you to do, you do it." He kept us from having to redo a lot of jobs, and it was largely because of him, and with God's help, that we finally began to get ahead.

A CHANGE OF ATTITUDE

After struggling with wanting to get out of business, finally one day, I thought to myself, "If we did sell this business, what would I do? This is what I know. I would probably be working for someone else doing the same thing." So I asked the Lord, "God, if you want me to stay here for the rest of my life, I will be content to do so. I just want your will in my life." Then I added "If you want us to sell this business, send someone in that wants it worse than we do." My attitude changed and I was happy.

We had two major accounts that kept us going during the years when businesses were folding. One was the Safari Magazine, and the other was the books we published for Byrd Granger. The two of them always paid their bills in a timely manner and sometimes in advance.

Things began to get better and soon we were actually in the "black." We began to make a decent income and

212

things weren't as much of a struggle. By this time, it had been about two years from the time we had put the business up for sale in the past. We were contemplating buying another printing press and some other equipment.

In order to compete in the industry, we had to upgrade which would be costly. It meant going in debt. We still owed a little over $40,000 on one piece of equipment, which we were making payments on. It would be a big step to purchase more equipment, and it was a hard decision to make. I began praying for guidance.

AND SUDDENLY...

About that time a real estate broker came in with a man that wanted to make us an offer on our business. They had found an old listing and hoped we would still be interested in selling. At first, we didn't realize how serious this man was and how much he wanted our business. By this time, we were making pretty good money and weren't real anxious to sell.

After we showed him some of our business records, we saw his enthusiasm mounting; we knew he wanted it badly. Bob told him to make us an offer. He came back with at least $100,000 more than we would have ever asked. In fact, a year prior to that, I would have given it to him. I remembered what I had said to the Lord about sending someone in that wanted the business worse than we did.

It turned out he was that man. That was January of 1991, and things began to happen very quickly. We agreed to carry the loan ourselves, and settled on a $50,000 down payment with monthly payments for the balance.

We needed to pay off the equipment, so we called for the exact payoff amount on our typesetter. It was originally $55,000 and we still owed approximately $40,000. It would take most of the down payment to pay it off; however, a very strange thing happened that

I will never forget. When Linda, our accountant, called the company to find out the exact balance, they told her we didn't owe anything. She questioned him further, repeating our company name, address, etc. He insisted we owed nothing. She requested that he send us a lien release, so we could clear the UCC with the State of Arizona, making it available to resell.

The release came within the week, so everything was clear and the final papers were soon ready to sign. We believe that was the favor of God and an absolute "miracle." There is just no other explanation for it. When God is in something, things can happen very quickly, and beyond our wildest expectations.

[Note: When I quit complaining and began to trust God, He was able to work on our behalf. God loves us so much and wants the very best for us, but our complaining is a form of unbelief, and can hinder our prayers from being answered.]

REFLECTION

The years of owning our own business, were very difficult years, but for me they were also "growing up" times, when I learned so much about other people; how to manage people, and deal with problems that involved people, and to deal with many of my own problems. I learned that if you want to be profitable to anyone or anything, you need to take care of yourself. If you're sick or in poor health you can't be your best at the mission God has called you to do. If we don't take care of our physical bodies, we could contribute to an early death before God's ordained time, and never complete the mission God has planned for us here on earth. We also are in no condition to help others, when we can't even help ourselves.

I never realized before that everybody was so different. I guess I had lived a pretty sheltered life prior to that. I never had to deal with the public. I always worked in a back room publishing house somewhere, and only answered to my immediate supervisor. All of these experiences helped prepare me for the job God had in store for me in the future.

It was very hard for me, when I began to realize how people lied so much and did such unethical things. It affected me in a way that is hard to explain. I felt I had become contaminated, after being exposed to a world that wasn't as pleasant as I thought it was; somehow it changed me. I didn't feel as good about life anymore, or even about myself, or smiling as much. There just wasn't that much to smile about.

I continued to seek God, and little by little, I began to learn how to deal with things. I decided to forgive the entire human race for just being who they are. Since Adam and Eve, we are all born with a sin nature. Only God can change that nature at the "new birth." We cannot expect sinners to act like Christians, but we can require them to obey the law. I learned that I could be who I was, in spite of the world around me. It was a good time of learning in my life, and I wouldn't trade all my experiences for anything. I learned to see and accept the world and people for who they are – some very precious, some very devious, some very truthful, some liars, some with God, some without God. They are all God's creation, and He has commanded that we love them all.

"A new commandment I give unto you, that ye love one another; as I have loved you, that ye also love one another." (John 13:34 KJV)

WHERE TO GO FROM HERE

"For as many as are led by the Spirit of God,
they are the sons of God."
Romans 8:14-15 KJV

After selling the business in 1991, I worked for a few months at Safari Club International on their 1,000 page Trophy Record Book; I went there in March of that year. It had to be completed, printed and delivered to Reno, Nevada, by January of 1992, for their annual convention. The deadline was crucial, but it got there on time. Afterward, I stayed there until about the end of May of 1992.

We put our house up for sale right after selling our business, and a few people were beginning to show a lot of interest in it. We were undecided about whether to stay in Tucson, or move to the Prescott area. We already owned our house in Dewey, and it was completely furnished. We had used it for weekend trips, but hadn't really thought about when we might permanently move there. I really did some praying about what to do, and asked the Lord to just open the doors that he wanted us to go through, and close doors we weren't supposed to go through. I really needed some spiritual guidance right

217

now, as we still had family in Tucson, so moving would mean leaving everything and everyone.

We had signed a non-compete clause when we sold our business, which meant that we couldn't work for another printer within 100 miles, so we were leaning toward moving, but that meant selling our house.

We had been back and forth to Prescott over several years. In 1990, I put in employment applications, throughout the year, at a few businesses, but there really wasn't much going on especially in Prescott Valley at the time. There was a fencing company, a Taco Bell, the *Why-Not Lounge and motel*, the *Tastee Freeze,* and the famous landmark Indian Tepee on Highway 69; that was about it. During the end of the year, nearly everything shut down from Thanksgiving 'till after New Year's.

While still working at Safari Club International, I was contemplating going into a different type of business. I was very much interested in computers and was just learning by trial and error how to fix them and exchange parts. There was a weekend seminar in California, teaching computer technology and repairs that I had applied for and planned to attend in November of 1991. We decided to combine our trip to Dewey, cleaning up the house there after my step-mother had moved out, and going from there to California for my seminar the next day.

We had some remodeling done on the house, and it was time for us to paint and begin to furnish it. After arriving, a storm began to roll in and, not really knowing what the news was, we were busy painting and watching it snow outside. It was beautiful, and continued to snow heavily all day. By the time we went to bed that night there were several inches of snow but not an extreme amount.

The next morning, we couldn't believe what we saw; it was the heaviest snow storm in years. In Dewey, there

218

was 19 inches of snow and in Prescott, over 2 feet. We had to be in California by 3:00 p.m. that afternoon, and it didn't look like we could get out. After a while, Bob put chains on his truck and went down to the small store at the corner of Highway 69 and Kachina Rd. By this time, the sun was shining, and the highways were already looking pretty clear. The snow plows had been through and the grocer said the highway should be clear by noon, all the way out of town, so when Bob came back, we got ready, and off we went.

COMPUTER SCHOOL

When getting to California, the class was everything I had hoped it would be. I learned a lot, and wanted more than ever to get into that line of work. Each student had their own computer to work on, and the first thing we did was go over the names of all the parts, comparing them to those listed and shown in our book. Then he told us to take them all out of the computer and strip it clean, including the power supply. He had us spread the parts out on our table. We even had to take all the key caps off the keyboard. Next, it was time for lunch, and we needed to be back in an hour. As I left the room, I looked back. Wow! It looked like someone had trashed it. I wondered if we would ever put things back together again. I thought to myself, "I hope no one gets my 'stuff' mixed up with theirs or bumps a table."

When we returned from lunch everything was just as we left it. During the course of the afternoon, I managed to get mine back together again, including the keys on the keyboard. Some students couldn't find all their parts. I don't know what happened. The instructor had to come up with some extra parts to help them. In order to pass the course, everything had to work again like it did when we first got our computers. Mine did! I was so glad.

One word of wisdom he gave us was, that if we were ever going to purchase a used computer, don't go to a rental place, no matter how good the prices seemed to be. That's where schools get their computers for students to work on. The store had no idea why they were renting so many.

SELLING OUR HOME

Well, back home again in Tucson, we began negotiating with three potential buyers for our house. Finally, one of them qualified and came up with the down payment. They just seemed to be the right people to sell to, so the deal was made. We had 30 days to move out. It was a much larger house than the one in Dewey, so we gave furniture away to anyone that needed things. We gave as much as possible to our kids, but there was still a house full.

Right after the house sold, we came to Dewey with Gordon and Anita, a couple of friends that lived next to us in Tucson. It was over the three-day memorial weekend of 1992. The day before going back, we were eating at a small restaurant in the area, and Anita had picked up the *Prescott Sun Newspaper.* She was looking at the want-ads and told me there was a listing for a typesetter at the newspaper – maybe I should apply for the job. I looked at the date and saw that paper was two weeks old. "I'm sure it's filled by now," I said, so I didn't get too excited about it or call them as they all tried to persuade me to do.

The next morning, we were all packed and ready to leave. All three of the others kept insisting I call the newspaper before we left, to see if the job was still available. Finally, I called them, and they asked if I could please come in and talk to them before leaving to go home, so I did.

A JOB OPENING

It turns out that they had hired a girl, but she wasn't working out, and with my experience they were very anxious for me to come in and talk to them. I had already checked out the going rate for jobs in the area, and at that time, anything over $6.00 an hour was considered very good pay. When the owner asked me how much I wanted, I hesitated, because I wasn't sure what I needed to say. I didn't need to have a large amount, I just needed to work somewhere for at least the next five years to get in enough time to draw as much as possible of my Social Security benefits, when I retired. While I hesitated, he said "how about $7.00 an hour to start, along with full insurance benefits. After three weeks, if things work out okay, I'll raise it to $8.00 an hour." I said "it's a deal." We shook hands; he took off and told the office girl to get my information, and set up my work schedule.

He wanted me to come to work immediately, but I insisted that I needed two weeks, so we set my start date at June 15, 1992. When we got home, I packed up as many clothes and personal things that I could think of, and whatever else would fit in my little Mazda Protégé and took off for Dewey. I never saw our home in Tucson again. Everything had happened so fast and fell into place so perfectly, I felt this was definitely a door that God had opened. I'm glad my friends and husband pushed me into making that phone call.

Bob was left to finish packing and empty the house. Over the next month, he made three trips with his truck and trailer, bringing *stuff* up here, including my piano, a large freezer, a very, *very* heavy safe, along with so much more. I don't know how he ever loaded and unloaded those items by himself, but he did.

There was an upholstery business just behind our place of business in Tucson. The owners had become good friends of ours, and Bob knew they went to the

221

big "swap meet" every weekend. Toward the end of the month, when he realized he was running out of time, Bob asked them if they would come in and empty out the house in exchange for everything that was left. There was still a lot of furniture and small household items. They agreed and emptied it in no time. To this day, I believe some of our photos and other small items disappeared in that transaction, but overall nothing has really been missed. The final inspection and walk-through went well, and we were moved.

REFLECTION

When a major change suddenly happens in your life, it is usually hard to know which direction to go from there. I had to trust the Holy Spirit to guide us in the right direction.

Many people come to me to pray with them about what they should do or where to go next in their lives. The first way I pray is that God will open the doors that I'm to go through and close any doors that I shouldn't go through.

The first time I came to Prescott looking for work, there were no open doors. I went everywhere and no one was even taking applications. The timing was not right at that time. The second time, after our house had sold, the first place I called was so anxious for me to go to work, they would have had me start the next day if it had been possible. The salary was good, the benefits were great; it was a good working environment. All lights were green. To me, that is what I mean by "open doors."

Don't get impatient. Be willing to wait for God's timing.

"For in due season we shall reap, if we faint not." (Galatians 6:9b KJV)

Chapter 4

JOURNEY CONTINUES

THE PRESCOTT SUN NEWSPAPER

❧

"Trust in the Lord with all your heart, and lean not on your own understanding; In all your ways acknowledge Him, and He shall direct your paths."
Proverbs 3:5-7 NKJV

The *Prescott Sun* was a fun place to work and I learned how to operate MacIntosh computers which were very different from the machines we had in our business; ours were much more sophisticated. Prescott in those days was "a little behind the times," to say the least. We had a fax machine in our home, and no one in Prescott was using them in 1992. When I saw how all the sales people had to run all over town taking proofs of ads, I asked why they didn't put in a fax machine. The answer was: "No one else in town has one to receive the copy." We had been using them for years in Tucson. Through the next six years that I worked there, I saw a lot of changes, and helped make a lot of them happen as well. I learned a lot of new ways of doing things, as a newspaper operates very differently from a small print shop.

A HEALING MIRACLE

While at the *Prescott Sun* everyone discussed their problems with each other. It was like a close-knit family. One day, Deb, my immediate supervisor told me that her daughter, Dulce, was in the hospital in Phoenix, with pneumonia, and they didn't know if she was going to make it. She had leukemia and was in a very weakened condition. She had been fighting it for some time and the doctor hadn't given them much hope. She also was engaged and had hopes of getting married, but her doctor told her she would never be able to have children. She was less than 20 years old at the time.

That night, I had a dream or vision, and I saw Dulce in bed at the hospital. I was standing at her bedside. She was asleep and I prayed a simple, quiet prayer, not wanting to wake her. After praying, I heard a voice say "She's well." I knew she was healed and going to be alright.

The next day, when Deb was talking about Dulce's condition with great concern in her voice, I told her about my dream. At first, I didn't know whether I should tell her the dream or not, but thought it might give her some hope. She was so excited and latched on to that hope with all her being. Later that morning, her mother called and was crying. I heard Deb say, "Mom, don't worry, Ann had a dream last night that Dulce was healed and is going to be okay." Her faith was amazing. Dulce did get well, almost overnight, much to everyone's amazement. Dulce was also healed of her leukemia, and soon was married to her fiancé. They eventually had two healthy boys. I met her years later in the post office with her boys, at about 10 and 8 years of age. She was still well and happily married. I continued working at the Prescott Sun for another year after my hip replacement surgery in 1996, and at the same time continued to help the food bank, as much as possible.

MY FIRST HIP REPLACEMENT

While working at the newspaper, I had to take time out to have a hip replacement, in August, 1996. It was one of the most frustrating times of my life, being home bound for eight weeks, and not being able to get up and go as I had been used to doing. One day, when I was sitting in my chair, I turned off the TV and began to pray. I said "Lord, if I ever get up and out of this chair, and back on my feet, I promise to never waste my time, and sit and do nothing for the rest of my life." My determination is to honor that commitment 'til I draw my last breath; however, as I get older, it is sometimes hard to distinguish the difference between resting and doing nothing.

ANOTHER ANGELIC MIRACLE

Kathy was still in a supervisory care home in Phoenix, Arizona when we first moved to Dewey, and I had to make several trips back and forth for visits. Eventually, we got her relocated in a Group Home in Prescott Valley, Arizona, called Aires, which proved to be an excellent place for her.

On one of my trips coming home from Phoenix one Saturday night, it began to pour down rain. It was monsoon season, and some of those storms can be horrendous. This was that kind of storm. I was on the last leg of my trip from Cordes Junction to Dewey, they had been working on the road and there were cones in the middle of the road, the area you could drive on was very narrow and rough. Many people were heading home to Phoenix, and the glaring lights coming at me through the rain were like a solid stream, as far as you could see.

Suddenly, the heavens just opened up and rain was so heavy I could not see even the car's tail-lights directly in front of me. I knew there was a car in front of me, but I could no longer see anything except blinding headlights from the other lane. I couldn't pull over as there was a mountain edge on the right and rough rocks where they had dug things up. I prayed and asked God to please help me and guide me, because I couldn't see where I was going. It was a very scary and frightening feeling.

The next several minutes were like a dream or a trance. My car just seemed to go of its own will, as I just sat there and knew God was in control of my car. Soon, I safely arrived at a gas station in Humboldt. I knew God had sent his angels once again to protect and guide me.

KATHY GETS A WORD FROM GOD

Once while Kathy was still in Phoenix, she had a woman that had come to the door of the group home where she was staying and talked to her about God. Kathy was in a different Group Home organization than the one she is in now in Prescott Valley, and they never took them to places they wanted to go, like they do here, so Kathy had not gone to church for several years. I knew Kathy missed that in her life, so when this woman wanted to come to her and hold Bible Studies, Kathy let her come.

Later, Kathy told me about the situation, and I, of course, wanted to know with whom the woman was affiliated. Kathy didn't know, and she couldn't remember a lot about what they talked about, so I thought it would perhaps be okay for a while, but I asked her to find out what church she went to, and to call me if anything seemed odd or different from the things she had been taught in the past.

It was hard to talk to any of the staff about what was going on, because they were so busy with the other two clients that were in very severe condition, that they almost ignored Kathy and probably didn't even know about the woman or who she was. Kathy had a walker and could get around on her own and the others could not, so she was pretty much ignored.

Another week went by, and Kathy said the woman didn't tell her what church she went to, but asked Kathy if she would like to go to her church, that she would come and pick her up. Kathy was calling to ask me if I thought it was okay. I was so torn about what to tell her, because I knew how much she missed going to church, so I just told Kathy to pray and ask God for guidance.

Toward the end of the week, I was curious about what Kathy had decided, so I called her and asked her if she was going to go with the woman. If she said yes, I would at least require the woman to give her an address. I didn't have to go that far, because Kathy said, I prayed about it like you said, and I remembered a scripture in the Bible about false prophets; I think this woman was a false prophet. I told her I didn't want to go with her.

I don't know why I was so overwhelmed with joy about her getting a word from the Lord, after all she is one of His. I am convinced after that experience that no matter what our mentality is here on earth, God knows how to reach each one of us, when we ask anything of Him. We are the ones that have a hard time communicating with people that are very different from us, but God knows each one of us personally and knows how to reach us, no matter what category man has placed us in.

THE WEEKLY NEWS

Sometime about 1999, Melody Reifsnyder and I started our own newspaper called the *Weekly News*. I was still working for the Prescott Sun, and was doing the production on the *Weekly News* in evenings and on weekends. It was first known as the *Tri-City News,* before I became a full-time partner with Melody. We were able to run ads regularly for the food bank that I had become affiliated with, and advertise all of their events and fundraisers.

The food bank continued to grow, as our newspaper continued to struggle. Not only did I do all of the production of the paper, getting the flats to the newspaper by 5:00 p.m. every Friday night, but also did the billing and distribution. After coming back from delivering the flats to the press, I would come home, eat something, and go to bed, only to wake up when I got a phone call about 11:00 p.m. that the papers were ready to pick up. Then I would get up, pick up the papers, then pick up Ben, Melody's 13-yr. old son, to help me deliver them. We drove all over Prescott, Chino Valley, and Prescott Valley, dropping bundles at certain drop-off locations for the next morning. We would finish about 4-5:00 a.m. I would then go back to bed until about 9:00 a.m., then go in to the food bank. By this time, I was putting in a lot of hours at the food bank.

Melody and I continued our newspaper for about a year and a half, and finally decided we just couldn't make it and had to close it down. The good part is that we were able to promote Yavapai food bank with free advertising during that time, and it helped build recognition and stability for them.

REFLECTION

Looking back, I can see that the things I learned at the *Prescott Sun* were a big step forward in the direction God was eventually taking me. I learned a lot about newspaper advertising, graphic software, and other things that were very different than general printing for the public.

I was also able to witness and "sow some seed" into those around me while there. If that had been the only purpose I was there, it would have been worth it.

It was also a time of refreshing for me to be working for someone else, and not having the responsibility of managing the business.

When my health problems flared up with my hip, and some other minor ailments, I was able to get them resolved quickly. I had great insurance benefits that paid well.

The incident of Kathy getting a word from God, just like He does for me, was so thrilling. It makes me to realize how much He loves each one of us, and is just waiting for us to ask of Him, so He can answer us. Our mentality doesn't limit Him. He knows each one of us and just how to reach us.

"For the eyes of the Lord are on the righteous, and His ears are open to their prayers;" (1 Peter 3:12a NKJV)

I was so thrilled to finally get Kathy moved to Prescott Valley. At the place she is living now, they take her shopping once a week, take her to church on Sunday, as well as, other places she needs to go as well. The people in the home are Christians and it is a much better environment. It is the first time in her entire adult life that I have not had concerns about how she is being taken care of.

The partnership with Melody running the *Weekly News* was also a great learning experience, and even though it was not very profitable, financially, it served its purpose well. I learned that you can't value everything in terms of dollars and cents.

VOLUNTEER WORK

"And whatsoever ye do, do it heartily,
as to the Lord, and not unto men;"
Colossians 3:23 KJV

When we first moved to Dewey, Bob took a couple of years off from work, since he was retired. During that time, he restored an old Volkswagen, painting it a bright Christmas red; it was a beauty.

He got to know all the neighbors, and also became a volunteer at the Prescott Valley Police Department. In those days there were a total of five officers, including the Chief, who was Ed Seder at the time. Only three officers were on duty at the same time. His first big job was to organize and clean-up the evidence room. From that he did a little of everything, and really loved being involved. There was hardly any crime in the area, and traffic problems weren't much of an issue either. The police department had more cars and "dummies" than they had policemen. They would park their police cars at certain strategic locations along the highway with a dummy in them, and it kept traffic pretty much under control.

[Note: Bob has continued his volunteer work at the Prescott Valley Police Department until the present time, and currently goes in two mornings a week and does finger-printing.]

His volunteer time at the police department didn't take up too much of his time and soon he was meeting me for lunch every day at work. He got to know everyone there. One day, my boss asked him if he wanted to go to work for them. He began selling advertising and meeting business people in the community, just what he always loved to do, and he made a little money besides.

Meanwhile, right after moving to Dewey, I started looking for a church home. I found one in Prescott Valley that was operating out of their home and had just started up. I wanted to go somewhere close, so I decided to try them. The first Sunday I was there, I was the only one there that wasn't part of the family. They were truly just starting their church.

I contemplated trying another church the following week, but after the service, they wanted to show me something else they were doing. They took me to a closet that had been remodeled with shelving and had it stocked with canned food. On the back porch they had a huge amount of pumpkins that they had just collected from Young's Farm. They were starting a food bank.

The pastor, Barbara O'Barr, was also a professional counselor. She said that one of the things everyone, that she counseled, had in common, was that none of the families had enough food. She thought if they could figure out how to get food donations, they could help those people.

I found Barbara and her friend, Judy Stewart, to be remarkable people with quite a vision to help people. I kept going to the house church, because it really intrigued me. I had never heard of a food bank before.

We were so consumed with our business in Tucson, I really didn't know there was such a need. Occasionally, I saw people on the street with their signs, but didn't take them very seriously. I honestly thought that most of them were probably scams. I think a lot of people feel the same way today, and sometimes they are right; however, I soon learned there *really is a need.*

As we began to move forward with the food bank, we learned of other places where we could get food, and also began to meet other agencies in the area. One day, Corky Archer, the director of "Church's Food Bank" in Prescott, contacted Barbara O'Barr and asked her if we would take over his food bank. He had a very bad heart and his doctor told him he needed to get out of the business right away. We all thought it would be a good idea as it was already incorporated, and we had no real structure established with ours yet. Corky and his wife were supposed to meet with us the next morning at 9:00 a.m. to have a board meeting, elect new officers and transfer all their paperwork and furnishings to us.

YAVAPAI FOOD BANK, INC.

The next morning, Corky and his wife didn't show up and we didn't hear anything until about 3:00 p.m. that afternoon. His wife called and said that "Corky" had passed away at 9:00 a.m. that morning from a heart attack. She came by that evening and we had our meeting. At that time, Bob and I, as well as Judy Stewart and Barbara O'Barr became the first members of the food bank's Board of Directors.

During that meeting, we voted to change the name, so it didn't sound like we just wanted to serve churches, or limit ourselves to just serving one area. Bob asked what the geographical area was that we wanted to cover, and Judy said "all of Yavapai County," so Bob said why don't we just name it Yavapai Food Bank – so Yavapai Food Bank was born. Little did we realize that this small beginning would grow to become our life's mission.

We were already outgrowing the small space at the home of Judy and Barbara on Etheridge Drive. The number of cars parked on the road every day was creating complaints from the neighbors, and was fast becoming a serious problem.

The police just turned their back on the situation, knowing we were trying to help people, but did come in one day, and asked us if we could space things out a little more so it would reduce the number of cars lined up on the road.

We inherited a lot of office furniture, shelving and "stuff" from Corky Archer that had been at their home. His wife wanted everything out of the house, as soon as possible. From her conversation, I think she felt the food bank killed Corky because of all the hard work.

MOVING YAVAPAI
FOOD BANK TO PRESCOTT

The food bank was well-known in Prescott, and nearly everyone concerned wanted us to keep it there. Mike Haywood & Associates in Prescott, offered us a small unit on Goodwin Street, next to City Hall, with free rent. We had desks, shelving and other items donated from various businesses, along with the things we already had.

I was working at the *Prescott Sun* during that time, and was able to get in a free promotional ad for the food bank, from time to time. Food donations began coming in and gradually it grew as people began to realize we were open. A few months later, Mike gave us an additional unit next door to the one we already had. More and more people were coming and we were soon outgrowing the second unit as well. The two units amounted to about 400 sq. ft. of space, and Mike couldn't give us any more. At the end of two years he merged his business with another developer and we had to move. They had plans to expand and couldn't offer us the free rent any longer.

We looked at several possibilities in Prescott, as we felt it was where we needed to be at that time, but couldn't find anything that was affordable.

FOOD BANK MOVES
BACK TO PRESCOTT VALLEY

After exhausting all possibilities for a location to move the food bank to another location in Prescott, Judy and Barbara finally decided to start looking in Prescott Valley for a location. The building at 8400 East Spouse Dr. had been a church, pastored by Everett Thomas, who had moved to a larger building, and started the Prescott Valley Food Bank. It was a duplex and one side of the building was empty. It was about 850 sq. ft., almost double what we had been using in Prescott, so it seemed like a large space to us. The rent was $500.00 a month and it was a tough decision to decide whether we could afford to pay it every month, but, after praying about it, we took a step of faith, and rented it.

We didn't have a large donor's base at the time and $500.00 per month was a real struggle. We moved in during the fall of 1996. By the time the holidays came, more donations came in than ever before. The really big breaking point was the first annual "Burning Desire to Feed the Hungry" food drive, held about three weeks before Christmas. It was sponsored by the Prescott Valley Chamber of Commerce, with Lew Rees as Director, and Yavapai Broadcasting, with Jackie Bessler. They spent the entire night in the park in the cold, with only a large barrel with a fire in it for heat. They also fasted the entire 24 hours of the food drive in memory of the poor. The food drive was advertised from the Safeway parking lot and they brought in a very large amount of food. Someone loaned us the use of an empty building, in order to sort the food. This was our first, and largest food drive, along with more recognition from the town. They did a lot of advertising on our behalf, and our food bank and donations continued to grow. We finally felt we could make it with such an outpouring of community support.

After the holidays, when donations slowed down again, we were still operating on a shoestring, so many times we had to send volunteers out to go from door to door to local businesses to try to collect enough monetary donations for our rent. By this time, I was doing all of the bookkeeping in the evenings, making flyers and other advertising, and still working at the newspaper full time.

After the first year at the food bank on Spouse Drive, we decided we needed more space and found out that the people next door were moving out. We wanted to rent the entire building which would be $1,000.00 a month.

The owner offered us an option to purchase the building over the next year. After much discussion and prayer, we decided to do it. It was a huge step for us, as it had been hard enough for us to come up with $500.00 a month and now it would be double.

A couple of years earlier, Judy had applied for disability, but it had been denied a couple of times. Her attorney had appealed again, and it was finally approved during that next year. She received $20,000.00, and said she wanted to go ahead and exercise our option and put $15,000.00 of the money down on the building. We all agreed to it, and also agreed that sometime in the future, if the money was there, that she would be paid back, even if just a little at a time. Since then, I am very pleased to say that Judy was paid back. It was a tremendously wonderful thing she did to help the food bank get off to a good start.

CREATING A CHRISTMAS
FOR A NEEDY FAMILY

A couple of years later, the food bank was able to consider helping at least one family in a special way at Christmas time. There happened to be a family coming to the food bank, at the time, that seemed to stand out above the rest, as far as need was concerned: she was a single mother with three small boys. She was trying to work at a part-time job, but just couldn't make enough to make ends meet. Her mother and some other friends had gone together and helped pay her rent, but there was not going to be anything for the children for Christmas. They needed clothes, shoes, and blankets desperately; the children were barefoot during the winter months. We contacted the mother and told her we would like to create a special Christmas for the three children and asked for their clothing sizes.

We then took them shopping at K-Mart. We purchased clothes from underwear to everything in between, and a nice warm coat and shoes. Then we let them pick out a special toy. The youngest boy was three years old. We asked him what he wanted for Christmas and he said a "Fwash wite." He couldn't pronounce his words clearly, but we finally figured out he was saying a "flash light." When this was confirmed, we said "Wouldn't you rather have a truck or something to play with?" He insisted he wanted a "fwash wite." I questioned him further, and asked why a flash light was so important. He answered in his childish voice "So I can see the bugs on the floor at night when I have to get up." I almost cried. He not only got his flash light, but a nice big truck as well.

The children were so excited about all that they got, and we were able to bless the mother with gifts as well.

That was just the beginning of what would become a Christmas tradition.

In recent years, we helped 250-300 families in one year to receive a special Christmas through our "Create A Christmas for a Child" program. People call in and get the names of a needy family and sponsor them. It has been a tremendous blessing to so many that otherwise might not receive anything for Christmas, because of their hardship circumstances.

WORKING AT YAVAPAI COLLEGE

Things were going fairly smoothly at the food bank, until I got a call from Yavapai College, asking me if I would come to work for them in their Marketing Department. Melody had gone to work there and specifically asked for me to work with her to promote the million dollar bond election, to expand the college and all their outlying campuses.

At the time, I felt the food bank was beginning to consume me more than I had intended, and Judy, the Director at the time, and I were having some differences of opinions in a lot of areas. So I thought it would be good for me to get "off the premises," for a while; I could still help with the bookkeeping in the evenings and help with fundraisers on weekends.

The job at Yavapai College ended up being a little over a year. During that time, I got very well acquainted with all the news media in the Tri-City area, by working with them and placing ads for the college.

When the bond election passed, and my job was over, they planned to place me in the Administration office, and I would be working under the Administrator, John Coomer. I really didn't think I wanted to stay on at the college, but Bob and I were both on Social Security by this time, and the extra income was pretty nice to have. Bob was also working for Galpin RV in

240

Dewey, selling motor homes, and we were doing pretty well, financially.

I was sitting alone at my desk meditating on what to do, and I just prayed a simple prayer, asking God for guidance. I remember saying that whatever His will for my life was from that moment forward, I was willing to walk in it. "Please show me the direction you want me to go."

Right at that moment, the phone rang; it was Judy Stewart. She got right to the point. She said "Ann, if you don't come back and take over as Director of the food bank, I am going to close the doors. My health is deteriorating very rapidly, and I just can't do this anymore." She had multiple-sclerosis, and evidently it was getting much worse.

Immediately, something inside of me leaped, and I thought, "God, I believe this is your answer." I knew there would not be any pay and perhaps not even enough to cover personal expenses, but I felt this was a direct answer to my prayer. Two years prior to this, someone had asked me if I would ever consider being the Director and I had said "Never in a million years." It's interesting how circumstances, and time can change your mind, especially when we feel it is a direct call from God.

I went in and gave my two-week notice, immediately. It was near Christmas and things were slow at the college at the end of December, so it turned out to be a good time to quit. I started on January 2, 2001, as the Executive Director of Yavapai Food Bank, Inc.

COMPUTER TRAINING SCHOOL

We started a computer training school out of the need to have someone help in the food bank office. At that time, most of our volunteers were people doing community service and most were computer illiterate. In the beginning, we had two extra computers that I had fixed

241

up just enough to get by, but a lot of people became very proficient on them. In time, our school grew and after a few years we had classes two evenings a week, along with high-speed internet, free of charge from *Cable One*.

REFLECTION

The first day I sat at my desk as the Executive Director of Yavapai Food Bank, I looked back over my life and was amazed that God would pick someone like me to be in such a position as this. I contemplated and prayed about where to begin.

I knew I couldn't handle this alone, so I asked the Holy Spirit to be my Senior partner in running the food bank, and I still depend on His guidance. I know I can't do anything without Him.

After the first year I went to Bob and asked him to quit his job at Galpin RV, and come join me at the food bank. There was too much outside running to be done, picking up food. He was the perfect person for the job. He was doing very well selling motor homes, and it was a big step of faith to get by on a lot less income per month, but I felt it was God's leading and knew we would be okay.

When I was young I had always been a shy and quiet person, not able to talk to people very freely. Many times, as director of the food bank, I am asked to speak on behalf of the food bank at different meetings for clubs or church groups. I can look back through my earlier years, and see where God has been preparing me for this position for over 35 years. My journey with the Holy Spirit has completely turned me around.

As the Director of Yavapai Food Bank, life continued to be busier each day. It is always a struggle to have enough food to meet the growing demands of those in need. Paying the rent, the electric, gas, and water bills are always a struggle, so I just keep praying and trusting God to help us, and He always does.

One of the things I determined, was to make Yavapai Food Bank a household name. You have to become known and keep yourself in the public eye. I remembered how Alpha Graphics had done it in Tucson when we were in business there. They advertised on the radio off and on all day long until you thought they were the only printers around. I knew we couldn't advertise like that, because we didn't have the funds, but we could go to every function in Prescott and Prescott Valley, even if it meant Bob and I were the only ones there. We would put up our little pop-up tent and table with our banner and greet people handing out brochures. There was not an immediate return for the time we spent doing those events, but in time, we became more and more recognized. I knew it was beginning to work when once we walked in at an awards dinner where many charities in the area were to receive a contribution; suddenly everyone clapped and someone shouted "There's Yavapai Food Bank – they're everywhere!"

It's amazing the confidence you can have in God when you know you're in the center of His will, and in the place where you're supposed to be. I still feel it was a divine leading of God that I was where I was.

HEART PROBLEMS

❧

*"My flesh and my heart fail; But God is the
strength of my heart and my portion forever."*
Psalm 73:26 NKJV

During my second or third year as Director of
Yavapai Food Bank, I began to start having chest pains.
When I went to the doctor he told me it was my heart.
I had clogged arteries and would have to either have
stents put in, or a bypass operation, and scheduled me
with a doctor in Phoenix to have it done right away. They
couldn't do that type of surgery in Prescott, at that time.

I was 69, and the first thing I thought of was that my
father died at 69 of a massive stroke, and my grandfather
died at 69 from a heart attack. Everyone had always told
me how much I took after my Dad and his side of the
family. Then I remembered, "NO, I am not subject to
generational curses! I've been born again, redeemed by
the Blood of Jesus, and no longer live under any curse."
I began to call Satan a liar and plead the Blood of Jesus
over my life. I said *"I WILL NOT DIE*, but live, according to your Word, Lord."

"I shall not die, but live, and declare the works of the Lord." (Psalm 118:17 NKJV)

Two years later, I had a second heart attack. I was in the emergency room at the time, and even though my pains had subsided momentarily, they were monitoring me very closely. About 9:00 p.m. I fell asleep and about 1:00 a.m., I woke up suddenly, with excruciating pains. The nurses and attendants were in there before I rang the buzzer. I remember saying "It's worse than a 10." (They had been asking me all night how I would rate the pain between 1 and 10.) She said "Honey, you're in the middle of a heart attack. You're going to surgery right now." The last thing I remember saying before I passed out was, *"Jesus, help me!"*

A few days after going home from the surgery, someone had told me about someone close to them, who had a sudden aneurism, and had died. Well, both times, after having five stents put in, I sometimes felt some strange fluttering or other strange symptoms, and I began wondering if the stents had slipped, or if something was wrong. I even began to wonder if I was building up to having an aneurism.

I was standing in the kitchen, and had TBN on TV. I was just listening to it in the background as I was working. While I was thinking these thoughts, about having an aneurism, suddenly a man began to speak and say something like "There's someone out there listening right now that has had some problems with your heart, and you are concerned that you are going to have an aneurism. The Lord just spoke to me, to tell you that 'you are not going to have an aneurism and that everything is alright.'" It came across loud and clear; *I grabbed on to it*, and I said "Lord, I receive it. Thank you, thank you, thank you!"

Two weeks later, when I went to see my heart specialist, they did an EKG and other tests, and he said,

"I can't believe you just had a heart attack. There is no indication whatsoever that anything happened; your heart shows absolutely no damage or change.

I believe when I called out "Jesus, help me!" that a miracle took place. He prevented my heart from suffering any damage, and confirmed it to me through the man of God on TV.

REFLECTION

After the second heart attack, I have been much more careful about my diet. My health is good, and I continue to trust the Lord to keep me whole and well each day, so I may continue the service He has called me to do.

"Your eyes saw my unformed body. All the days ordained for me were written in your book before one of them came to be." (Psalm 139:16 NIV)

God has ordained my days until my race is finished.

I will continue to serve and love Him, and serve and love His people while here on earth.

Our first building in Prescott Valley in December 2004 during our food distribution.

OUR MISSION CONTINUES

୨ৡ

"He hath dispersed, he hath given to the poor;
his righteousness endureth forever; his horn
shall be exalted with honour."
Psalm 112:9 KJV

In time, as the food bank grew, our little building on Spouse became smaller and smaller. We added a roof over the back and concreted all around the building for a parking lot; it was only dirt when we purchased it. Food had to be distributed from out in the back, under the long porch roof, where we had tables made to stack the produce. We also had added a sprinkling system, along with an evaporative cooler to help keep the produce cool and last as long as possible. We were storing other things on the one side of the building with tarps over them and also using rented storage spaces to sort food after food drives. Later, when Mike's Appliance moved from their building on Robert Rd., the building was empty for some time. During that time, Mike allowed us to use it to store and sort our food from large food drives. It was such a blessing, I don't know how we would have managed without it, since we couldn't afford to pay rent on another building. God gave us such great favor with the community. It made the difference with us being able to continue our operation.

About a year later, we finally had to rent additional space for the next two years. We rented one of the tri-plex buildings east of us on Spouse. We used it for our clothing outlet, and also to sort and store food from our food drives.

We still had our rented storage units for seasonal items, and things that we needed, but not on a daily basis. We put two rows of 18" shelves all around the inside walls of our building on Spouse, creating a little more storage space. We also had to store things outside under tarps, and in the additional building on Spouse east of us. We absolutely did not have an extra square inch to spare and didn't know how we were going to be able to continue operating under such difficult circumstances. We knew we had to do something, but with no money, all I could do was pray, and ask for guidance.

We had expanded the food bank to the entire building, but was quickly outgrowing it as well. We were soon operating out of at least four different locations, moving things around, trying to keep things running smoothly; everything was becoming nearly impossible. We desperately needed to be under one roof to operate effectively. Even if we had enough money, which we did not, to buy or rent a larger building, that was not the only problem. The proper zoning for a food bank also had to be considered.

We wrote letters to Fain Signature Group to see if they would be willing to donate some land to the food bank for us to build on, but they were not in a position to help us at that time. We looked and contemplated renting, but found that most of the places we thought were possibilities were not zoned for a food bank. A couple of years after the first letter, we wrote a second letter to Fain Signature Group with the same answer.

Then, one day, a couple came in to the food bank, and asked to come in to talk to me. When they did, they stated that they wanted to make a rather large donation to help us move into a larger building. They realized we had been struggling for a long time in a building way too small.

It seems that someone had died and left them a sizeable inheritance. Their tax accountant had recommended they make a donation to a charity, and he recommended Yavapai Food Bank. They gave us $40,000 which was the largest donation we had ever received, up to that time. It was not enough to purchase another building, but it might be enough to get something started.

We continued to look for buildings. Our search led us to the buildings on Long Mesa, since they were in the correct zoning required for a food bank. Initially there was only one building for sale in the area, but it was just too small, being about 4,500 sq. ft. We felt we needed a 9,000 sq. ft. building, but couldn't find one of that size in the correct zoning area, or that we could possibly afford.

A GLIMMER OF HOPE
FOR YAVAPAI FOOD BANK

After the food bank received the $40,000 donation to help toward a larger building, we had been looking everywhere for what we hoped would work for us. Finally, the place where we are now on Long Mesa became available. It was only 6,000 sq. ft. instead of the 9,000 we had hoped for, but by this time we were so desperate, it was either move into something larger, or face the possibility of having to close down the food bank.

The building was a cabinet shop and looked pretty run-down overall, but we could see potential. The next step, was contacting a banker to see what finances might be available. One of our Board Trustee members, Bill Lacy, suggested Tim Naylor, the banker he did business with through Chase Bank.

It looked impossible to me, but after a few sessions, much paper work exchanging hands, and much prayer, a contract was drawn up. We had to come up with a sizable down payment through a special fundraiser, much more than the $40,000. After praying about what to do, we entered into the contract, and immediately, put an appeal out to the community. We had three months to finalize things, smaller amounts of money came in here and there, but not nearly enough to make up the difference we still needed. We figured we needed $50,000 within a few weeks to finalize the deal.

I put a notice out and prayed for favor. The majority of us on the Board felt very good about the location of the building, and felt like this was what we were supposed to do. Days went by and nothing substantial came in.

One day, during our food distribution time, while I was gone on some errands, a couple came in the door, waited in line until they came up to the table where people were signing up for food. Vicki Sandoval asked if she could help them. The woman spoke up and asked "Is Ann Wilson in? We'd like to make a donation." Vicki told her I wasn't in at the moment but Bob was in. Meanwhile, the man began writing out a check and handed it to Vicki. She looked at the check and said "I'd better go get Bob. Wait here just a minute." She ran through the building and brought Bob up to meet them. The check was for $50,000, specifically designated for our building. The man was "Mert" Davis.

That was exactly what we needed. We were able to close the deal and move forward with our plans to refurbish the building. I can't even possibly remember how we raised all the money it took to get the building ready to move in, but when it was finished and I looked back over what we had spent, it was over $200,000. That included everything but the parking lot. The original price on the parking lot was $110,000. Fann Construction Co. was the contractor, and was able to get over $30,000 donated from different vendors. The balance came to $80,000. They went ahead and finished it and we were only able to pay $30,000.00 on it, when finished; they carried the rest. It took us a year and a half to pay it off. They were so patient.

The whole thing was such a miracle, how everything came together. The timing was perfect, and the money came in just in time. Once we had to hold up work for about two weeks until we had enough money to continue, but finally we were able to move in on June 2, 2008. We moved the entire operation over in four days, and never missed one food distribution. The last day at our building on Spouse was Friday at 3:00 p.m. and we were open by Tuesday the next week at 1:00 p.m.

If we had waited just three more months to purchase that property, we probably would not have been able to, since the economy went through a sudden down-hill crisis, and buying and selling of property nearly came to a stand-still. Many construction businesses in the Prescott area went out of business; building contractors and their crews were out of work. Things continued downward from that point onward and many more people lost their jobs.

The number of people coming to the food bank tripled in numbers over the next two years. We would never have been able to handle the growth from our small building on Spouse. We all believed it was God's provision and perfect timing.

Our plan was to put the building up for sale on Spouse to help pay down the building on Long Mesa, but nothing was selling, so at this writing, we still own it.

The new home of Yavapai Food Bank at 8866 East Long Mesa Drive in Prescott Valley

After cleaning it up to try to sell it, it remained empty for several months, then, because the clothing distribution had made it so crowded at our location on Long Mesa, we decided to go ahead and use the Spouse building, moving the clothing and computer school there.

It has always been hard to have someone over there full time so we have it opened only on Tuesday and Wednesday afternoons. We also set up tables, during our food distribution times at Long Mesa, of miscellaneous donated house-hold items for people to take.

YFB EXPANSION PROGRAM

One of the things I am trusting God for, as I write this book is for an additional 6,000 sq. ft. building, and our existing properties paid in full. With everything, including expanding the parking lot, it will amount to close to a million dollars, but I know that with God all things are possible.

One night, as I was driving to Life Christian University and praying and talking to God on the way, I was praying at the time for $24,000 to pay off our first parking lot by the end of the year. When I said that prayer, the Lord spoke to my spirit, and said, "Is that all you want?" I suddenly realized that I was limiting God, that no amount makes any difference to Him. I said, "No, Lord, I want that food bank completely out of debt." He spoke again to my heart and said *TRUST ME* ." At that time, my vision wasn't to expand our parking lot or add another building as we had just moved in. Since then, due to the down-turn of our economy, and so many people out of work, our numbers have tripled, and now we have almost as many people parking up and down both sides of the street, as well as, in our lot. The $24,000 that I had asked for by the end of the year, came in within three months, and we were able to pay our existing parking lot off by April of that year.

There was some land behind us that had been part of an old railroad track, and was in four small parcels. No one was using it, because it was land-locked and not much good for anything to someone other than us. It would be a way we could expand our parking lot if we could get ownership of it. I found out who owned the parcels and, initially, they didn't want to sell it, or donate it to us, as I suggested. Over the next two years, I contacted them from time to time, but to no avail, then one day, the accountant for the person that owned it, called and made an offer to sell all four parcels to us for five thousand dollars and they would pay all closing costs. It was almost as good as a donation, and I accepted immediately. We got the deal completed, the title changed over, and the land merged with our existing property within the week.

Since then, we have had our plans drawn up and approved by the Town of Prescott Valley, including a very expensive retaining wall to utilize as much space as possible. Mailers, with a cover letter, seeking help, a schematic of the plans, and picture of our crowded situation, have been mailed out to several foundations and businesses. Nothing has transpired as yet, but I know I heard God's voice, and I don't believe He would have prompted me to ask for more money, if He were not prepared to give it. I am trusting that He will provide the means for this project to be completed, in addition to getting our existing buildings paid off, or the one on Spouse sold.

We were able to add "temporary" parking on part of the area by creating a 4-foot wall, filling it in and leveling it on top with four inches of AB mixture and cement. The cost was much less than attempting to do the entire area. Temporarily, it has gotten a few more cars off the street and has helped, but in reality, it is only a band-aid compared to what needs to be done.

REFLECTION

The food bank story is a miracle in itself. It was started from a home in Prescott Valley to help a few struggling neighbors that didn't have enough food. The four of us on the first Board of Directors, never dreamed, at the time, it would grow like it did.

Looking back on our journey with the food bank, it sometimes seems like a dream. It has been a continuous stream of miracles, which brought us to where we are today.

By the time we moved to Long Mesa, Bob and I knew we were in this for life. Once you begin to see the need, and so many desperate families, you can't just turn your back on it and walk away.

When people ask me when I'm going to retire, I just say "When God tells me to leave, or I'm down and can't get up again." I guess I'll retire when I get to heaven; however God may have other plans for me – *even there*! In reality, I believe we're all going to be very busy. God is a creative God, and we're made in His likeness.

GRACE EVANGELISTIC MINISTRY

"Now he that planteth and he that watereth
are one: and every man shall receive his own
reward according to his own labour."
1 Corinthians 3:8 KJV

Grace Evangelistic Ministries, pastored by Barbara O'Barr, also had begun to grow, largely because of the food bank that was started in her home. Soon we began having the services in the Library in Prescott Valley. I began teaching the Sunday school; there were about a dozen children by this time. The children ranged in age from 2 to 12 years of age. It was a challenge, but we had some very good classes.

In teaching them about some of the miracles that Jesus did, the children were like sponges and so open to the teachings. During prayer request time, I decided to have the children lay their hands on the person who needed healing. I soon discovered that their faith was tremendous, and we saw many miraculous healings. One of the greatest was of my grandson, Harley. He was about 3 or 4 years old at that time and had some kind of infection and growth just under his chin. It continued to grow and the doctors didn't want to touch it for some reason. It seems they thought it could be something pretty serious, and possibly life threatening. I can't remember all the circumstances or what they said it might be, because they needed to do more tests. It looked horrible and his face soon swelled up very large. Parents were concerned about their children playing with him.

The children laid hands on him and prayed that it would be healed, and within 24 hours it began to drain, and the swelling gradually went down. Today, there is still a large scar there. He is 22 now. The doctors never did tell us what they thought it was, but God healed it anyway. Through this, I learned why Jesus said that we need to come to him as a little child; their faith is so great. They simply believe and don't have fear or other things that hinder their faith, as adults sometimes do.

"Then Jesus called a little child to Him, set him in the midst of them, and said, "Assuredly, I say to you, unless you are converted and become as little children, you will by no means enter the kingdom of heaven." (Matthew 18:2-3 NKJV)

I loved teaching the kids, and over the next 10 years, continued with many of the same children. It was a very rewarding time, molding their lives by the Word of God. We took them to nursing homes a few times. The children sang, and just went around and talked with people. We also took them Christmas caroling at several nursing homes and the VA hospital for a couple of years. It blessed the residents, as well as, the children. I wish we could see more people doing that sort of ministry.

Nearly all of these children came from homes where either one or both parents were alcoholics or drug addicts. At one particular time, every child in the class had one or both parents in jail or prison. Sometimes, they lived with other family members, including grandparents. Most of them had no transportation to get to Sunday School. We picked them up every Sunday morning. The first thing we did was give them something to eat since most of them came without any breakfast.

Barbara O'Barr and Judy Stewart moved the church from the library to the other side of the food bank building, for a couple of years when it became vacant. Even though the congregation dwindled greatly in the latter years, possibly due to Barbara's illness and other things, we continued until Judy also became so ill that she had to quit the food bank. They disbanded the church at about the same time, sold their house in Prescott Valley, and moved to Texas to be close to Barbara's children.

REFLECTION

After Barbara and Judy disbanded Grace Evangelistic Ministries and moved to Texas, I looked for another church home. I began going to Victory Worship Center on Jacque Dr. & Robert Rd. in Prescott Valley, just a couple of blocks from the food bank.

During the 10 years that I taught the children through Grace Evangelistic Ministries, I believe I grew as much as the children did. It was hard work, but very rewarding. I will never forget one particular boy. He was quite a problem child, having been "kicked out" of nearly every school in Prescott Valley, and had several other charges against him from a very early age. He was diagnosed as having ADHD. He continually disrupted the class, and it was a challenge for me to know how to work with him. His mother came to me one time and said, "Ann, if you want to kick him out of your Sunday School class I'll understand.; can't manage him myself." I said, "No, I can't do that. If he gets in serious trouble and ends up in prison or something, I don't want it ever said that he went astray, because he was kicked out of Sunday School, and besides, I may be able to actualy teach him something.

A few years later, I heard this young man was doing well, he got a job at a McDonald's and he had left home. I hadn't heard much about him again for a couple of years. Then, one day, he came by to see me at the food bank. He seemed to have his life together pretty well, and turned out to be a pretty decent sort of man. About a year later, he came in again, and introduced me to his fiancé, as well as, his new baby son. I asked him when they planned to get married, and told him he needed to do so as soon as possible, in order to assume his responsibility as a father and husband. He gave some excuse as to why they hadn't yet, but they were planning to marry.

I may never, in this life, see all the children that came to Sunday School through those years, but I hope I will see them all in heaven at a future time. I think of all of them often, and can only hope enough seed was sown in their lives to help change their futures for the better; I pray that they are living for God today. Some sow, some plant, and some water, but God gives the increase, as Paul stated to the Corinthians.

"I planted, Apollos watered, but God gave the increase. So then neither he who plants is anything, nor he who waters, but God who gives the increase." (1 Corinthians 3:6-7 NKJV)

COMING HOME

☙❧

*"He has shown you, O man, what is good; and
what does the Lord require of you but to do justly,
to love mercy, and to walk humbly with your God?"*
Micah 6:8   NKJV

BARBARA AND HARLEY

After moving to Dewey in June of 1992, the following Mother's Day in May, we drove to Tucson and moved Barbara and Harley up here. Barbara had called me that morning, wishing me a Happy Mother's Day. After talking to her, she related to me some of the hardships she and Harley were going through, including a drug-bust in the duplex next door, people running all over the roof and the place surrounded by the police, with lots of fighting and commotion. She said that she just sat on the bed holding Harley and prayed "God, please protect us and show me what to do." Two weeks after Harley was born, his father went to prison, so he was not around to help them.

After hanging up, I couldn't bear the thought of what they were going through. Bob asked me what I wanted to

Barbara and Harley
2007

Left:
Barbara and
Harley - 1995

Harley - 2009

Right:
Harley and
son, Travis
16 mos., and
Shawna
2013

do for Mother's Day. I answered him by saying, "What I would really like is drive to Tucson, pack up Barbara and Harley, and move them up here." In just minutes, Bob hitched up the trailer to his truck, and we were on the road. He knew I would not be able to rest without doing something.

Harley was 13 mos. old; Barbara didn't have a lot of furniture, and we packed everything we could in our truck and trailer, cleaned up the place, contacted the landlord, paid whatever she owed, and left for home with them with us.

They stayed with us for about three weeks, and we finally found an apartment for them, and we helped Barbara get a job at Taco Bell. She didn't have a car, so Bob got up at 4 a.m. every morning to go pick her up and take her to work.

About a year later, we found the property at 8858 Cheryl Drive, and purchased it so Barbara and Harley would always have a place to live. The trailer proved to have a lot of electrical problems and was not safe, so, in less than a year, we had to move the old trailer off the property and purchase a new mobile home to replace it.

Bob was so faithful at getting up every morning to pick up Barbara for work. He had never been a morning person, and I know how hard it must have been for him to do that. When God answered my prayer to give me someone to help me, I'm sure he looked a long way to find such a man; Bob never complains. When I first prayed that prayer and asked God to send someone into my life to help me, I had no idea of the things still ahead of me. Things that would be even greater than the ones I had at the time I met Bob, but *God* did.

BILL COMING HOME

About a year before, my daughter, Lynn, moved here from Florida, my son, Bill, moved here from

Bill in 2013

Washington. It was in February of 2010 when I got a phone call from him. I had only seen him twice, since he left home at 18 years old. One time, a few years after we built our house in Tucson, we made a trip to Washington to visit them, and Bob and Bill went deep sea fishing.

The second time, his family came to visit for a few days in 1985. Bill was 56 years old when he moved to Prescott Valley, so it had been quite a few years since we had last seen him.

When Bill called me, he said he was really sick and thought he was dying. He was too sick to work and he had no money. He had stopped drinking and was staying at his daughter, Amy's house, for a couple of days, because he had no place to stay. He couldn't stay there permanently, there just wasn't room.

Actually, Melissa, one of his other daughters, called us and put him on the phone. I know it was hard for him to ask for help, but I could tell by the sound of his voice that he was pretty desperate. After some discussion on our end, we purchased a ticket, and had him on a plane the next morning. He was here that afternoon and we had him admitted to a men's recovery center in Prescott where he stayed for six months.

While he was there, they helped him sign up for AHCCCS through the Department of Economic Security, and got him enrolled with a primary care physician. They also helped him get his Driver's License through Arizona, and took him to his doctor appointments. He was almost blind in one eye and found out he had really bad cataracts. He was able to get that taken care of, as well as, other medical issues while there.

When he got out of the recovery center, we found a place for him to stay, and he began helping at the food bank as a driver. He looked for other construction work, but there was not much regular work in the area at that time. Since then, he has continued to work at the food bank, not only driving, but also taking care of the grounds, like watering plants, keeping the weeds under control at both food bank locations, and has become a real asset to the food bank.

REFLECTION

When our children call for help, it is like when we call out to God for help. We must respond in love to our own; I remember when my father helped me. Families must help each other. It is a terrible situation when there is no family to help; I have seen many such cases.

Our children are always our children, no matter what the age. God loves us unconditionally, and we should love the same way. All God wants from us is to call on Him when we need help. He is right there with out-stretched arms; He is all forgiving, and anxious to give us all good things that pertain to life and happiness. Parents and other family members should do the same.

With so much heartache and trouble in the world, we all need someone at some time in our life to say "Come on home – everything's going to be okay!" My father did it for me when I was in a desperate situation, and we should always remember to do the same for others when an opportunity arises. I was so thrilled when Bill called me and asked for help. He is such a joy and blessing to our family, I can't imagine life without him.

TIME OUT FOR A HUNTING TRIP

"Thou makest darkness, and it is night: wherein all the beasts of the forest do creep forth."
Psalm 104:20 KJV

Bob and his brothers have always been avid hunters, and after we were married I started going with him on hunting trips. Finally, I got my own license and tag and began to hunt as well.

On one of our trips, after I had shot an elk at about 5:45 p.m. in the evening, Bob had dragged it, with his quad, to a place where he could get it later with his truck. The sun was going down rapidly, and in less than an hour it was completely dark. You couldn't even see the moon for the trees. If you've never been in the woods after dark, you will never realize how "spooky" and dark it can be. If there is anything dead, the wildlife will come in and clean it up, to where you can't even tell where it was by morning.

Well, since the elk was too big to put on the quad, Bob had to drive the quad back to the road where we had left his truck, and also call for some help to get it loaded in the truck. It was 265 lbs. of meat after it was dressed out, the largest any in our hunting group had ever taken to date.

I and my flashlight stayed with my elk. In years past, when I was much younger, I would have been too scared to stay there alone, but now I had no fear whatsoever. I had a great time; I started doing a flashlight dance and I began to dance and sing. I thought about the movie "Dancing with Wolves," and thought to myself, "He has nothing on me." I knew those animals in the bushes wanted that elk so bad they could almost taste it, but I hoped they would be more frightened of me, dancing around. There is no one else in the woods late at night, so I didn't feel I was bothering anyone, and I just sang and danced until Bob returned.

I also had my cell phone, and at about 8:00 p.m. Shari, Bob's daughter, called me from Phoenix, and asked what I was doing. When I told her she laughed and laughed. She knew we had gone hunting and thought we would be back in camp by that time of night.

Well, finally, by about 9:00 p.m., Bob came back in his truck with our friend, Harold. After they "field-dressed" the elk, we got it loaded in the truck, then took it to Flagstaff. It was midnight by the time we got there. We have a friend in Flagstaff that has a meat packing plant to which we always take wild game. We called ahead of time and he left the key outside the cooler room. We were able to hang the animal on the pulley outside, skin it and clean it, as much as possible, then roll it inside on the pulley, until he was able to finish dressing and packaging it. Another friend in Flagstaff was Kerry Ketchum who was director of the Northern Arizona Food Bank for many years. He helped us several times when we killed an elk. All we had to do was call him, and he was right there. He is a powerfully strong man, originally from Oregon, and an avid hunter. We were always so blessed to have him help us when we needed someone. God has blessed us with some awesome friends.

REFLECTION

When I was a child I wouldn't even step outside the door after dark. I really had forgotten all about it, until I suddenly realized I was in the middle of the woods alone, after dark, and I wasn't afraid. I knew the Lord was with me wherever I was, and I had no fear.

BARBARA'S BATTLE WITH ALCOHOL

✂

*"The thief cometh not, but for to steal, and to kill,
and to destroy: I am come that they might have
life, and that they might have it more abundantly."*
John 10:10 KJV

Barbara continued to work at fast food places, and soon she was working at Burger King. Judy Stewart happened to be the manager there, at the time. It had not been apparent to me that Barbara had a serious drinking problem, until Judy began pointing it out. Even then, I wasn't sure whether Judy wasn't making it bigger than it was. Barbara was very subtle with her drinking, and, as we discovered later, she had been drinking almost continuously, a little at a time, all day long for years. It was the same way her grandfather on her father's side drank; he never got really drunk, but always had to keep a whiskey bottle nearby. It became very obvious at times, but she was clever at her attempts to hide it and always denied she was drinking.

The years took its toll on her health, and by the time everyone knew she was drinking heavily, no one could seem to help her, nor could she help herself. She went in to *Hillside Care Center* for a while and got sober, but it only lasted about a year. She began having more serious health issues, but her doctors couldn't really work with her, because she continued to drink. At some point, she also began using drugs, and it looked as if her life was hopeless.

I really began praying more earnestly than ever, and one night, after she had been arrested, and it looked like she was headed for prison this time for child neglect, I poured my heart out to God, and groaned and travailed in the Spirit until I thought my stomach was going to turn inside out. I remember specifically asking God, that somehow, "Whatever it takes, please set her free from her alcoholism and help her turn her life around." I knew that it would not be just Barbara that would go through it, but I would go through it with her, and I would do all that I could that would be necessary to just see her completely delivered.

The next morning, her lawyer called and said that Barbara was going to be released. The judge dismissed the charges, she didn't know why and no one knew, we still don't know why. I believe it was God's intervention. If she had gone to prison the sudden withdrawal from alcohol could have killed her.

That was when Barbara agreed to go to *Blessing A. Ministry*, which is a women's recovery center; hopefully to receive the help she needed. That lasted about 30 days or less, because she drank, broke the house rules and had to leave.

After that, it was just one problem after another until she got another DUI, the one just a little over five years from the first one. The judge sentenced her as though it was a second one, *within* five years, because of the extreme circumstances. Her alcohol level was so high that her doctor said most people would have been in a coma before it could get that high.

Because of the strict laws in Arizona, she was sentenced to nearly four months in the County Jail in Camp Verde. It was over a month before she had to start her sentence, which would hopefully be long enough for her to detox from alcohol. During that detox period she had hallucinations and extreme paranoia; I wondered if her mind had been completely destroyed. She was also fined over $11,000 in addition to paying $60 a month while in jail, $2.00 a day for meals, and extra for anything she needed from the commissary, plus charges for phone calls. In addition to that, when she did get out, her driver's license would be suspended for at least five years. At any time, if she was ever reported taking even one drink, it would be a violation of probation and she would automatically go back to jail.

After she began her sentence, she still had a lot of physical problems; her hands were shaking, and she slept most of the time. She hadn't really established a good primary care doctor on the outside of jail, so they had no pre-instructions as to how to treat her, except they knew she was an alcoholic. The doctors didn't know the extent of her liver damage, nor did we at the time.

She got sicker and sicker, and finally, one Sunday morning, after I got home from church, at about 11:00 a.m., a doctor from the Camp Verde Medical Center called me and asked if I had a daughter named Barbara Passfield. It seems that she went into a coma while at the jail. They thought she was dead. She got a release from the judge; they took her and all the possessions she had and rushed her to the Camp Verde hospital on December 12, 2010. The doctor said things didn't look good. She was in a coma and not expected to live; they had a "do not resuscitate" order on her paperwork. I immediately called Theresa deSoto, because I knew she had gone to the early service also. I asked her to pray, that I was headed to the hospital; she said she would meet me there.

275

When we went into Barbara's room, you could feel the spirit of death. There was nothing I could do and nothing I could say; God had given me the assurance of Barbara's deliverance. I sat down and began to sing "Amazing Grace." Theresa joined me, and then we sang another song, and another. That's all we could do; I couldn't say any appropriate words. I knew God was working, and that she would not die, but live. Several years earlier, God gave me a scripture in Psalms 112:1-3, that I continue to stand on concerning my children and trusting in Him; I knew all was well.

"Praise the Lord! Blessed is the man who fears the Lord, who delights greatly in His command-ments. His descendants will be mighty on earth; the generation of the upright will be blessed." (Psalm 112:1-3 NKJV)

When Bob came in later, the doctor called us aside to talk to us. He said there wasn't much hope for Barbara, that her liver was so damaged that if her heart stopped or her kidneys failed, they would not resuscitate, as it would just be bringing her back to a life of pain, and a longer, drawn out time of dying anyway. Bob spoke up and said "We believe in miracles." The doctor looked down at us in an intimidating fashion and said, a little sarcastically, "Well, that is what it will take." I was so proud of Bob for speaking up to that doctor. You can't intimidate Bob, and we couldn't accept the doctor's prognosis.

The hospital did a good job of treating her, getting her ammonia levels down, and after about three days, she began to come out of the coma. She was pretty shaky and wobbly for about a week or more afterwards. She got out of the hospital on a Thursday afternoon, and insisted on going to church that Sunday. I had to help her out of the car and steady her to be able to walk inside, but she was

276

determined to get to church. By this time, she knew she had a close call with death, and I think God did a miracle in her spirit while she was in that coma.

Barbara's primary care doctor sent her to a very good liver disease specialist in the area, and he really seemed to care about Barbara. He was a Christian, and seemed to understand the battle Barbara was going through, which was a battle she would fight for the rest of her life. He offered words of encouragement, and as he worked with her medically, God continued to work with her spiritually.

There were a lot of bumps in the road, but our hopes were higher than ever, that she would completely regain her health. Even though the doctor said that the liver would never restore itself, she would always have to adhere to a very strict diet and stay on medication if she wanted to live, I knew that *"with God all things are possible."* (Matthew 19:26)

Almost a year later, after she was more stable, the judge said she had to finish her sentence. We knew this would not be easy on her, but the judge made sure her doctor communicated with the jail on just what medicine she was to take and when. The doctor at the jail had to agree to adhere to everything her doctor had said was necessary, even if she had to be put in the infirmary during the entire time.

We were all very apprehensive about it, but Barbara said she prayed before going in, and asked the Lord to help her get through it. She said he spoke to her and told her "to arm herself;" she knew what that meant.

When she got there, at the first opportunity, she asked for a Bible. She spent as much time as possible in the Word, and it sustained her. After two and a half more months, she came home on December 24, 2011, with her sentence of jail time behind her. She was a brand new person, a *"new creation in Christ Jesus."*

"Therefore if any man be in Christ, he is a new creature: old things are passed away; behold, all things are become new." (2 Corinthians 5:17)

The second time she got out of jail, she was determined to be baptized again. She had been baptized as a child, but now it was much more meaningful to her. She was baptized at the next baptismal service in May, 2012, as soon as she was a little stronger.

By the next school year, Barbara enrolled in Life Christian University, and after a year and a half, came within two months of finishing her second year and earning an Associate's Degree. She attended church regularly, and was baptized in the Holy Spirit; however, she still fought her liver disease, having to have several pre-cancerous polyps removed in her stomach over a few months' time, while still going to school.

Someone had to drive her everywhere she went. Her doctor's appointments were many. Her doctor told us that she would have to be checked for stomach polyps at regular intervals, for the rest of her life. This is one of the things, as well as, hemorrhaging in the stomach that usually leads to death. The last time he checked her stomach, the report came back negative for any sign of them. We continued to believe God that they were "finished," gone and would not return!

Lynn helped a lot by picking her up for church and helping with some of the running around. Bob picked up her medication, and the whole family had jumped on the bandwagon in support of her efforts to recover.

I knew when I prayed that "gut-wrenching" prayer that I would have to do my part in helping with her recovery; having my daughter back was worth more to me than all of it.

While going to the university, Theresa deSoto encouraged Barbara to go back to school to get her GED, so she could upgrade to a Degree student. Barbara went and completed the course, and took her final exam with very high test scores. We were all so proud of her and all her accomplishments over the two and one-half years after she came home from the hospital.

She would be walking with her graduating class through Life Christian University on June 8, 2013, with an Associate's Degree in Theology. Life looked good and hopeful.

We found Barbara an apartment right across the street from the food bank, and that in itself was a miracle. Long before she went to jail the first time, I prayed about that apartment becoming available, and just knew that was the one we were supposed to have. Almost every day I looked to see if there was a "For Rent" sign, but nothing. I was tempted to go ask the people if they were planning to move, but resisted. Meanwhile, we looked at several other apartments, and finally, found one that we thought would work for her. I was supposed to go talk to the people about it at noon, but on the way to the food bank that morning, I said I'm going to look at that other apartment one more time, and when I pulled up in front, there was a "For Rent" sign out front; it had just gone up. I knew that was the answer to our prayer. We called, asking to rent it, before they even advertised it. With the apartment just across the street from the food bank, it made it much easier for me to run over there if needed. Our God is a great and awesome God!

Jan Haas, a close friend of Barbara's, had just lost her house, had no job, and nowhere to go. I asked her if she would be willing to move in with Barbara to help keep an eye on her, help with the cleaning of her apartment, do some of the cooking, and take her to the store when needed. In exchange for a free place to live, a small monthly stipend and gasoline money, she agreed to do so and it was working out very well.

Over the next year or more, there were a couple of "emergency" moments, but the doctor gave us advice of what to do and she got through them.

About 5 or 6 weeks before her final emergency, some of us had begun to notice that Barbara was not her usual self, all the time. She began missing church and school a little more often, due to some very painful hemorrhoids. She also mentioned having more increasing pain in her stomach than she had been. She stopped coming over to help at the food bank for a couple of hours a day during the food distribution. Her doctor offered some treatment for her problems, but things were still "off and on." She couldn't take any pain pills or a lot of other things, because her liver was so bad. She was still supposed to adhere to a very strict diet, which is very hard to do over a period of years.

Barbara had been doing so much better when she came home from jail the last time, that Jan, who had been living with her, had begun to make plans with her own life, and decided to move out. I considered getting someone else to move in with Barbara to help, but Barbara insisted that she wanted to try things on her own. Jan had been doing most of the cooking, and because it was just Barbara now, she began to take shortcuts and eating sandwiches and things not on her diet. According to her doctor, she was not supposed to have more than one slice of bread a day, and it should be well-toasted at that.

On the day of her GED completion, she picked up a strawberry pie from the food bank and said "I'm going to go home and celebrate." I cautioned her not to eat the whole pie (ha-ha). She was so happy, I didn't want to spoil her joy. It's possible that some of the deviation from her good diet possibly caused more pain and deterioration of her liver.

On June 7, 2013, Barbara had an episode where she had to be taken to the emergency room at Yavapai

Regional Medical Center in Prescott Valley, and, as before, I felt sure she would be okay.

Her son, Harley, and her friend, Branden, got to go in and see her for a few minutes and talked with her. At that time, she was very coherent and able to talk. Then Bob went in and also was able to talk with her; finally, Pastor Randy and I went in. By this time, they had just given her some type of coma inducing drug, but we were assured she could still hear us. We both said prayers and words of encouragement to her.

The drug they gave her was to help them put a breathing tube in, just in case she had trouble breathing during the helicopter flight to Phoenix. Her doctor felt she could be better treated at the Banner Samaritan hospital, where they had more high-tech equipment and specialists. We were told we wouldn't be able to see her for three or four hours after she arrived there, so we followed by car and got down there about three hours later. I was expecting a good report.

When we got there, the doctor came out immediately to talk to us. Things didn't look good, but I still felt she was going to be okay. It wasn't until the doctor told us that her heart had stopped for 10 minutes, soon after she had gotten there, and even though they got it beating again, he appeared very concerned. Then he looked at me very somberly and said, "Just to be absolutely honest with you, I don't think she will make it." My first inside reaction was "No, I will not accept that." I tried hard to hold on to my faith, but when the doctor told us that if she lived she would have extensive brain damage and probably have no motor skills and unable to talk. Suddenly I thought to myself "This is it; she's run her race. This is the finish line." I went over and prayed in her ear. I don't know if she could hear me or not, but I just simply prayed "Lord, if Barbara can't come back to us completely whole, please take her on home to be with

281

Barbara at Kay & Aaron's
wedding

Barbara at Lynn's Tea Party
2013

Barbara's last photo taken
May 2013

Barbara 50th Birthday Party,
May 15, 2013

you." She lasted about another two hours, and late that night on June 7, 2013, Barbara got her final graduation diploma from the King of Kings, Jesus himself. When she left her body she went home to be with Jesus.

"Therefore we are always confident, knowing that, whilst we are at home in the body, we are absent from the Lord:... We are confident, I say, and willing rather to be absent from the body, and to be present with the Lord." (2 Corinthians 5:6, 9) KJV

REFLECTION

Alcohol is such a debilitating substance. It destroys so many lives, of both those that drink, and those around them. Barbara expressed to me many times how much she hated what alcohol was doing to her, but she just couldn't quit.

One night, just before she was arrested, she told me she had just prayed "God please help me somehow. I just can't help myself anymore. I am totally out of control." She felt her arrest, later that night, was an answer to her prayer. Even though she couldn't conquer her addiction on her own, she was always asking God for help.

She told me after she came home from the hospital, that just before she went into that coma, she prayed "God help me!" He heard her, and He did. I believe a miracle took place while she was in a coma. She came out of it a "new creature in Christ Jesus."

An interesting thing happened at Lynn's house in Prescott Valley the day Barbara died in Phoenix. About the time the doctor told us that Barbara's heart had stopped beating for about 10 minutes, Lynn was just getting home from work, and suddenly she felt a whisp of a sort of movement with a "playful" spirit about it. Without thinking she said "Barbi, you get back in that body." It surprised her when she heard what she said. It happened so fast. She said she thought she "felt Barbi's presence." At that time, she didn't know that her heart had stopped or that she was as serious as she was.

About a month before Barbara's passing, I had a dream of her. I saw her completely whole and healed. She had lost a lot of weight, not skinny, but just healthy looking and beautiful. When I awoke I just "knew she was going to be completely healed," and I would see her just like I had in my dream. I believe death is the ultimate healing, and I will see Barbara again just like in my dream. In fact, that's how I see her now.

I will always consider it a special gift from God that he brought Barbara out of that coma the first time, and gave us two and a half good years of seeing her completely changed and free.

"Therefore if the Son makes you free, you shall be free indeed." John 8:36 NKJV

Thank you, Jesus!

ANGIE COMES FOR A VISIT

*"And be ye kind one to another, tenderhearted,
forgiving one another, even as God for
Christ's sake hath forgiven you."*
Ephesians 4:32 KJV

Several years later, after moving to Dewey, Angie, my granddaughter who had lived with us for about a year when she was 15, and her friend, Rich, came to see us.

Since we saw her last, she had married, and had five more children, two of whom were twins. Her husband had been arrested and sent to prison. Her children were taken by CPS and put in a foster home, and eventually were put up for adoption. We learned later that they were adopted by a Christian woman who kept them together through the years.

Angie was about 25 years old when she came to see us. Her main purpose was to ask our forgiveness for all that she had put us through when she was a teenager, and especially to apologize to Bob. He had a hard time forgiving her, because she had continued to lie to him about something, he had given her every opportunity to tell the truth about, and she wouldn't; he gave up on her.

285

Angie and Rich - 2013

Angie had just found out that she had Hepatitis C and thought she was going to die. She wanted to make things right. She asked to go in to see Bob privately, which she did. I still don't know the essence of their conversation, but she came out in tears, but peaceful looking, and he seemed very mellow. I think it must have gone well. When we stepped outside, I asked her if she knew Jesus as her personal Savior. We had talked to her several times in the past, but she just didn't seem to know what we were talking about at that time, and not ready to make any changes. This time was different, she broke down and started to cry, and said she didn't know how or what to do. I led her in a prayer, having her repeat it after me. I advised her to start attending church when she got back home in Tucson, and to call me any time if she had any questions.

A year or so later, we got a call from Rich saying that Angie was in the hospital in very serious condition. She had gone to the hospital with excruciating back pain. Later the doctor admitted that she was in such bad shape he didn't think she was going to live more than couple of days. Her spine was deteriorating, and two of her discs were eaten away. He prescribed a body brace for her and when we went to see her in the hospital, she was able to bear the pain, as long as she wore the brace. She had to wear it 'round the clock.

After the doctor saw that she did so well with the brace on, he prescribed her to be placed in a nursing home for a year, and on strong antibiotics for the osteomyelitis. She had to wear the body brace all the time except for bathing.

When I first told Bob about her having osteomyelitis of the spine, and that two of her discs were eaten away, he commented, "She will fight it all of her life." He said that, because of his sister who broke her leg when she was 10 years old, it had never completely healed. Sometimes

—— Angie's seven children ——

Megan - 2013

Breanna - 2008

1998 - The last time I saw Angie's five children from
her marriage to Dell, before they were adopted.
Left to Right: Jessica, Wyatt, James, Chris, and Alix

Jessica - 2014

Wyatt - 2014

Alix - 2011

it would get better, only to flare up again later, worse than before. It was always a battle. When he said that, something inside of me rebelled against that comment and I said, *"NO,* she will not. She *WILL* be well!" I said it so emphatically that it almost startled me. It was like it came from somewhere deep within me, before I even realized it. I know it was the Holy Spirit, and I believe Angie was healed from that moment on.

Even though she stayed in the nursing home for several months, she kept saying she felt like she was okay. Finally, after about nine months, the doctor decided to take another MRI and see how her spine was doing. He also had scheduled surgery for her to go to immediately afterwards. When he looked at the MRI, he appeared surprised, and called to his nurse to cancel the surgery appointment. It was as though she had never had any problem whatsoever with her back; it was perfect.

She was miraculously healed of osteomyelitis of her spine, with bones being totally recreated. I told her at the time, that I believed God healed the Hepatitis C also, and she felt it too, but it wasn't confirmed until many years later when going in for a checkup. Her doctor couldn't believe that she had a problem with her spine or her liver. She sent for the MRIs to prove it to him. He could hardly believe it. She had no sign of ever having had a problem with either.

REFLECTION

I was so glad that Angie came to see us to ask forgiveness. It was a strong indication that she was really trying to set her life straight, and the years following proved it to be true. I believe she went home, a new person that day after we prayed.

It was a very sad thing for her to lose all her children, but I'm glad she made the choice of adoption. Far too many women make the wrong choice when they find out they're expecting a child, and it just doesn't seem to fit into their plans at the time.

All of Angie's children who were put up for adoption, so many years before, have started coming back into our lives in 2013. Megan, Angie's first child, found Lynn on Yavapai Food Bank's Facebook page, and Angie found her third child, Alix, the oldest of the five, on Facebook. She also has visitation privileges with Breanna, her second child who grew up in Sahuarita, Arizona.

The second girl of the five, Jessica, called me one night at home and introduced herself. She had just turned 18 and had moved out of her adoptive parent's home, and was sharing an apartment with another girl. The last time I saw her she was two years old. We met Wyatt at Jessica's apartment in May 2014. He is living in Flagstaff and came down for a visit. At this writing, we have not seen the twins, James and Chris, but have hopes that we will meet them again soon.

Later, when Angie went through the problem with her back, her faith proved still to be strong. I was so full of joy when I heard of the doctor's report and the findings on the MRI of her back that I couldn't contain myself. One night, when going to the University, I was walking across the parking lot just as Robert Stack was also crossing the parking lot. He said, "Ann, is that you singing?" I didn't even realize I was still singing after getting out of my car. God wants us to be full of joy. He wants to give us even more than we can imagine. We just have to ask and believe. I thought about the following scripture in John.

"Hitherto have ye asked nothing in my name: ask, and ye shall receive, that your joy may be full." (John 16:24)

At times, life has some very pleasant surprises.

Chapter 5

❧

RETIREMENT YEARS

GOD HAS NO RETIREMENT PLAN

ی‌ک‌ک‌

*"But none of these things move me; nor do
I count my life dear to myself, so that I may
finish my race with joy, and the ministry which
I received from the Lord Jesus, to testify to
the gospel of the grace of God."*
Acts 20:24 NKJV

When I first started going to Victory Worship Center, I noticed a flyer about Life Christian University (LCU). Their headquarters was in Tampa, Florida, but they sponsored an extension campus at their church. It sounded interesting, but I really thought I was too old to go to Bible School. I had a lot of teaching over the years, and didn't feel it would be that beneficial to me because of my age. I was 68 at the time.

After a few months of going there, one of our daughters, Shari, got in trouble, and had to serve some years in prison. While there, she asked me if I could send her some Christian literature, books or something. The church worked it out where she was able to take the Bible Course through the Rhema Prison Ministry. When it was enrollment time again in the fall, Linda Boaté, the pastor's wife at Victory, asked me if I would like to enroll, that way, I would know what Shari was studying at the same time, and I might be of some help to her. It sounded like a good idea, so I enrolled. I first planned to start as an audit student, but Bob Leonard, one of the instructors, convinced me that I should apply as a Degree student, so I did.

I did my practicum hours teaching Sunday School and cleaning the church. Ellie Kent and Robert Stack were my fellow students. Ellie and I went every Saturday and cleaned the church together. We just had three in our class, and after the first year, I was hooked; what a tremendous experience! I was, of course, anxious to go on to the second year, but Linda became very ill, and they decided not to continue the school the following year. I was devastated, as were the other students, especially those going into the fourth year, and planning to graduate.

Over the summer, Robert (Bob) Leonard, who had been one of the instructors for the school, began going to Living Faith Church on Coyote Springs Rd. in Prescott Valley. Through Pastor Randy Vanesian and Barbara, the church secretary at the time, they were able to start up the extension campus, at that location, by the time school started the first week of September.

It was amazing, and nothing short of miraculous how everything came together in such a short period of time. By September, everyone that had been attending at Victory Worship Center was able to continue school at the new location.

I was still attending Victory Worship Center and teaching Sunday School there. The Sunday School program had changed, and it began to be more difficult for me to fit in with their new program. I wanted to continue to teach, but felt I just couldn't conform to their style of teaching, and became very discontented.

I called Pastor Randy at Living Faith Church, and asked him if I joined his church, did they have any teaching positions open. He assured me they did, and I decided to make the change. Now I was going to school and attending the same church again. It was a much better situation.

MY STUDIES THROUGH LCU CONTINUES

Meanwhile, I was continuing my Theology studies through LCU. The second year, had a course called "Discovering Your Purpose." This was very frustrating and challenging, because, by now I am nearly 70 years old. I had no idea what I would be doing "five years from now," and other similar type questions. I almost decided to quit school at this point, because it was a course geared for a young person. My husband, Bob, kept encouraging me to continue. Finally, I decided I would approach this as though I am going to live forever, and just "dream" anything I imagined I would like to do, so I went for it, and continued onward.

We had a computer training school through the food bank, which I had been teaching at that time, and I had always wanted to take some students further and teach them to be technicians. I decided if I went to college, and took some further training I could introduce this program through our computer school, so that is what I put in my Destiny Planner. I continued to fill it out according to my current desires and plans, and got an "A" on my final exam; however, God had other plans for me that I was not aware of at the time, or even imagined would ever happen.

During my third year, Bob Leonard, who was the current Dean and Director of the school at that time, asked me if I would be interested in teaching the next fall. I told him I would, but he had also asked three others, and he picked the one that had already graduated with her Bachelor's Degree. I was fine with it, and was looking forward to taking the fourth year as a student anyway. Ellie Kent and I had become great friends, and we wanted to finish school together.

Sometime in late July, Bob Leonard came to me again and asked if I would teach the first month for him, which would be the third year class. He had been having some heart problems, and he needed to have some tests done. He wasn't sure if he would be up to teaching the first month in September. Of course, I agreed to do it, and as the month progressed, he seemed to get worse, and they had to delay the tests. Then he had another heart attack, and things were continually delayed; his health seemed to be going downhill. What started out to be one month, ended up being the entire year as teacher. Many of us in the church, as well as at the main campus, were praying for him, and I felt certain he would be coming back.

Meanwhile Shelly Ellis, who was an instructor, as well as, the school administrator, was feeling a lot of pressure, since the entire load of the school suddenly fell on her shoulders, with Bob Leonard's illness. I began helping her, especially with the advertising, ordering the school books, making the CDs from the recorders, and other things. I studied the Director's handbook and took the test so I could officially be her assistant.

Bob Leonard finally decided he was going to have to quit as Dean of the school. Shelly and I continued to run it as we had been doing. At the end of that year, we had a meeting with Pastor Randy and he asked us to decide between us what rolls we would take. We decided I would be the Dean, since Shelly had already been doing the administrative work and preferred it. I would be in charge of ordering books, taking care of the accounting records, the graduation ceremony, and other things that Bob Leonard had handled. She would continue with the administrative work, sending in the grades, and be the contact person with the main campus as necessary.

We were still praying that Bob Leonard would recover, and be back with us soon. He was not able to come to the end of year commencement program that year, as we had hoped he would, nor did he make it back the next school year.

About two weeks before he died, I had a very vivid dream. I saw him walking rapidly, with a spring in his step and a broad smile on his face; he seemed a little taller, thinner, and younger. The words "completely whole," was what came to me as to how he looked; his smile was definitely *his smile*; he was carrying his Bible in his left hand as he walked. As he went by, he just glanced my way for a moment, waved and smiled very excitedly, like someone in a hurry, on a mission, and didn't have time to stop and talk. I remember thinking he must be going to teach somewhere and was in a hurry to get there.

When I awoke, I thought surely he had been healed. The next morning, I called Dawna, his wife, and asked how he was doing. I expected a good report, but instead she said he is much worse and going downhill rapidly. He didn't have many good days after that, and I believe my dream was showing me his perfect healing.

REFLECTION

When this temporary tent finally falls away and our Spirit is released, we are eternally with Jesus, and really begin to live.

Bob Leonard always talked about a special message God had given him when he was ill, and he was looking forward to teaching it. I believe he got his opportunity and many more.

The last summer he was with us, and as he and I were standing in the church auditorium, talking about the future of the school, I said something like "My dream is to see this auditorium full of first-year students." He replied, "I can see the mantle has passed." That's one of the last things I can remember him saying to me personally.

Well, from that point on, I officially became the Dean of the school, and continued teaching.

All of us that knew Bob Leonard will always be grateful for the vision he had in starting the LCU Prescott Valley Campus, and also for Pastor Randy, who shared his vision and allowed it to operate under the umbrella of his church.

Since God has no retirement plan, I am grateful for the journey He has taken me on, and the inevitable journey still to come.

DUAL RESPONSIBILITIES

୬᧞

"It is God that girdeth me with strength,
and maketh my way perfect."
Psalm 18:32 KJV

As I continue to work every day at the food bank, teach and prepare lessons for the school, I feel I am right on track with my destiny. When I look back at my "Destiny Planner" during my second year of school, I was a totally different person compared to five years later. My goals have changed, and my only desire is to disciple, and teach others; to see their lives changed, set ablaze with the fire of God burning in their hearts. I also continue providing food and other help for the growing number of people in need that come to the food bank.

There are times when the demands of the food bank, and the school coincide, but God has placed many people in my path to help me. Vicki Sandoval was with us for many years, and was my right-hand person until the end of June 2012. Due to health problems of both herself and her husband she had to quit.

My daughter, Lynn, moved here from Florida in June of 2011. She gave up a good job in Florida just to come

Lynn with Bob at Halloween Western theme event at church -

home and help me, especially with Kathy and Barbara. While looking for work, she began working as a volunteer at the food bank. When Vicki had to quit a year later, Lynn was able to step into her position. I didn't realize how much I needed her until her skills and talents began to emerge. I had no idea she could do so much. She had been gone about 30 years, with a one-day visit with her friend Cathy in 2000, and a visit in 2004, when Bob and I went to Florida to visit her for a few days. Now, I would hate to try to get by without her at the food bank.

Harold Henry who is our warehouse manager came in as a volunteer two days a week, and then full time. He was also definitely a "God send" to us, as well as, the many other volunteers that make the food bank what it is.

I believe that everyone that has come to the food bank to help us has been sent by God in answer to many prayers. The most skilled and very highly qualified people have all come in as volunteers, and are probably better skilled people than I could have ever been able to afford, if I had set out to hire them.

When we needed a new "Intake Person" at the front desk, Maureen Henry, Harold's wife, quit a very good job in Prescott, and came to fill the position. Her skills, expertise, and caring personality is the most ideal person I could have ever asked for.

At our LCU campus, Shelly Ellis was very efficient with the Administrative work, however, after another year we decided she needed an assistant. We asked Theresa deSoto if she would be interested in the job. After the first year of assisting her, Shelly turned the job over to her. Theresa and her husband, Andy, did an excellent job over the next year as the school continued to grow. The following year, the job once again went back to Shelly, and after a few months, when Shelly was not able to continue, Lynn, my daughter, took over the job as the school administrator in addition to the work she does at the food bank.

In 2013, I felt God was leading me to Chaplain service at the local hospital. Just prior to that decision, I had an experience with an individual who was dying. I went over to her home to pray and talk with her. She had led a very full Christian life and was ready to meet Jesus face to face; she died about a week later. It was a very moving experience, and I felt I wanted to help more people through their moments of illness and distress, and being a Chaplain at the hospital might be an avenue in that direction.

At this writing, I am a volunteer Chaplain at Yavapai Regional Medical Center (YRMC) East campus two days a month. It is an extremely rewarding job.

REFLECTION

When God calls you to do something, He always makes sure you have the abilities, skills, and tools to do it, and sends in the people necessary to help.

I love the direction God has taken me. I know he has directed my path and I continue to trust in Him for the strength, and ability to do the work He has called me to do.

God has directed me in ways that I never thought or dreamed possible this late in life, but I realize that as long as I have breath, I am a servant to mankind, with the help of the Holy Spirit working through me.

He has ways of preparing us for service. I had already taken two Chaplain courses through Pastor Ray Petersen at our church, never thinking I would ever have time to pursue such a ministry, but just wanted to know more about it. When the desire came to fulfill the call to be a Chaplain, I was already prepared.

I have always thrived on being on the edge of being "too busy." Age and energy sometimes slows me down,

302

and I have to take a few more naps and let others do a little more, but I know God's grace is sufficient for whatever He calls me to do, and my resolve is to continue to work until God calls me home.

"For I know the thoughts that I think toward you, saith the Lord, thoughts of peace, and not of evil, to give you an expected end." (Jeremiah 29:11 KJV)

TEACHING – MY GREATEST PASSION

❦

"Finally, there is laid up for me the crown of righteousness, which the Lord, the righteous Judge, will give to me on that Day, and not to me only but also to all who have loved His appearing."
2 Timothy 4:8 NKJV

I am so thankful for the opportunity to teach in my later years. Being the Dean and an instructor at the LCU campus in Prescott Valley, has been one of the most fulfilling times of my life. I am always asking God to give me a special word for the students, and one early morning, as I was still lying in bed and meditating on the Lord and on my lesson for that night, the words "jointly fit together" suddenly came to me.

I saw a box of a thousand piece jigsaw puzzle before me. There was a beautiful picture on the box of a small cottage with white shutters near the edge of a forest. The sky was a perfect blue with white clouds, and in the yard a flower garden with some beautiful red roses and other plants. I remembered when I was about 6 or 7 years old, when I was trying to work on a puzzle for the first time with my older brother and cousin. I was trying to force pieces into the wrong places. My brother told me "Don't try to force it if it doesn't fit – it won't come out right." I thought about the words "jointly fit together," and realized this was similar to the lesson Paul was teaching concerning the body of Christ.

> *"...but, speaking the truth in love, may grow up in all things into Him who is the head — Christ — from whom the whole body, joined and knit together by what every joint supplies, according to the effective working by which every part does its share, causes growth of the body for the edifying of itself in love."* (Ephesians 4:15-16 NKJV)

> *"Now ye are the body of Christ, and members in particular. And God hath set some in the church, first apostles, secondarily prophets, thirdly teachers, after that miracles, then gifts of healings, helps, governments, diversities of tongues. Are all apostles? are all prophets? are all teachers? are all workers of miracles? Have all the gifts of healing? do all speak with tongues? do all interpret?"* (1 Corinthians 12:27-31)

In meditating on these things, the Lord showed me that too many people want to be like other people, trying to copy their ministry, or wishing they were like them. God has a separate calling and plan for each of us, and when we aren't content to be in the place where He puts us, nothing comes out right. If the blue sky wants to be like the red rose, it would look out of place in the middle of the sky, and so forth. We all have to find where God wants us and be content to operate in our specific calling. There is great power when we are unified as one body working together ... and it is beautiful!

LOVING THE TRUTH

Something else I've learned is that we not only need to know the truth, but we need to love the truth.

"The coming of the lawless one will be in accordance with the work of Satan displayed in all kinds of counterfeit miracles, signs and wonders, and in every sort of evil that deceives those who are perishing. They perish because they <u>refused to love the truth</u> [emphasis added] and so be saved. For this reason God sends them a powerful delusion so that they will believe the lie and so that all will be condemned who have not believed the truth but have delighted in wickedness." (2 Thessalonians 2:9-12 NIV)

Satan knows the truth, but hates it, because he is the father of liars. He is the great deceiver and if we don't love the truth we can be led away by our own desires and lusts of the flesh. Satan is always there to deceive those he can. Loving the truth will prevent us from being deceived.

"But each one is tempted when he is drawn away by his own desires and enticed." (James 1:14 NKJV)

According to Psalm 116:165, people that love God's law, which is truth, have great peace.

"Great peace have they who love your law, and nothing can make them stumble." (Psalm 119:165 NIV)

The following scripture also tells us how we can make our calling and election sure and never stumble.

"But also for this very reason, giving all diligence, add to your faith virtue, to virtue knowledge, (6) to knowledge self-control, to self-control perseverance, to perseverance godliness, (7) to godliness brotherly kindness, and to brotherly kindness love. (8) For if these things are yours and abound, you will be neither barren nor unfruitful in the knowledge of our Lord Jesus Christ. (9) For he who lacks these things is short-sighted, even to blindness, and has forgotten that he was cleansed from his old sins. (10) Therefore, brethren, be even more diligent to make your call and election sure, for if you do these things you will never stumble;" (2 Peter 1:5-10 NKJV)

Verse 10 tells us what to do so that we may never stumble. Notice the things he tells us to do in verses 5-7. When we do those things we will make our calling and election sure, and will never stumble. God never tells us to do anything we are not able to do. It takes staying submitted to His will, and daily working at adding these things to our life.

"I can do all things through Christ who strengthens me." (Philippians 4:13 NKJV)

Chapter 6

REMINISCENT THOUGHTS

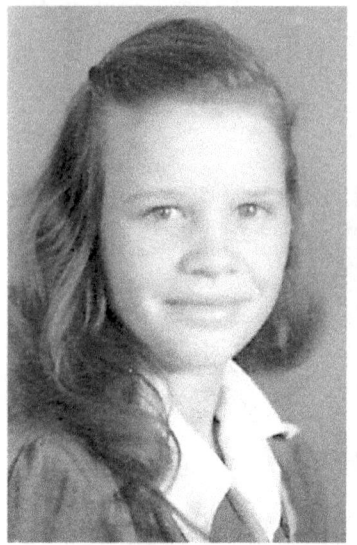

Ann 1946 - 6th grade   Ann - 1945 - 5th grade

Steve, Ann, Mary, David - 1947, the   Ann, Mary, and David,
year we were rejoined with my Dad.   1945
(Sorry to cut you off, David,
there was no more picture)

SOME IMPORTANT EVENTS
THAT HELPED DIRECT MY PATH

When I was in about the second grade, Pearl Harbor was bombed. My dad was 39 years old at the time, with four children and didn't qualify for the draft; however he enlisted anyway, along with others. The whole nation was up in arms and every able-bodied man wanted to go fight, and protect our country. It was one of the most patriotic eras in my lifetime.

While he was gone, Dad made arrangements for the younger three of us to live with a close friend of his and his wife. My older brother lived with another family that had a son about my brother's age.

After we were with this family for a few months, things weren't going so well with them and they were talking about getting a divorce, so she sent us to stay with her mother. Her mother was a fine Christian woman that instilled in me a deep love for God and a desire to go to Church and Sunday School. She read the Bible to us every night. We also went to Vacation Bible School every summer. She was a beautiful seamstress, and made me wear dresses which I didn't like. I had always been such a tomboy and felt more comfortable in levis, but I learned to tolerate the change in my life style.

311

She was very heavy, and couldn't get around well, so I learned to ride the bus everywhere. I ran errands for her and was able to get myself, my brother and sister to church by riding the bus. I also did the grocery shopping which was right across the street, and helped take care of my brother and sister. I learned to do house work and sew. When she got an electric sewing machine, she gave me her old Singer treadle machine to put in our bedroom. I learned to make everything on that machine. I had the best dressed dolls in town, and later learned to make most of my own clothes, which I have done throughout my life, as well as for my children. She also gave me piano lessons and eventually hired a more advanced teacher for me. Even though we were with her for only four years, it was enough to get me really started in the right direction.

One of the things I remember that she always told me was "that whatever my hands found to do, do it with all of my heart as unto the Lord."

"And whatsoever ye do, do it heartily, as to the Lord, and not unto men;" (Colossians 3:23)

She said that if I did my work to please God and not just to please man, I would automatically find favor with man as well. It proved to be true all of my life.

At an early age, while still living with her, I learned that neighbors would hire a person to do yard work or other chores. Sometimes they would hire me to baby sit, even though I was still pretty young, I was very responsible. I liked making money and I sometimes spent a little, gave a little or spent some on someone else, but always saved a little. I always had money after that and it was a good feeling. She taught me the principle of tithing, and it was good to have an offering when going to church.

I have always remembered her admonitions and advice and tried to live by those standards throughout my life. When I look back I can say that I truly was highly favored on every job I ever worked at. I learned that working was a type of creativity that could be fun and exciting, and I always wanted to learn more and more.

One of the things I specifically remember was when I was in my second year of high school. We had moved to a house that hadn't been lived in for some time. The owner's wife had died and the landlord moved out of the house into a small trailer out back, and had just let everything go. Weeds were three and four feet high; with all the brush you couldn't tell what was in the yard.

When we drove in the driveway, I yelled "I get the yard!" It was in the worst condition possible, but I loved cleaning it up. When I finished with that yard, we discovered there were rose bushes, flowers, other bushes and trees in the midst of all that brush. Everything looked like a beautiful garden when I was finished. The irrigation that we got from time to time kept the grass green, and I loved to sit out in the yard on my blanket and read, or just watch the cars go by. It wasn't really work to me, because I loved doing it, and seeing the beautiful transformation. When I get to heaven I want to find this woman and thank her for all she taught me that helped mold and direct my life during those years I was with her.

Because of this experience, I know how important it is to teach children when they're small. The things a child learns during their "innocent" years will mold their character for life. I wish all teachers could see this vision, and realize how important their ministry is.

Another one of my favorite foundation scriptures is the following:

"I beseech you therefore, brethren, by the mercies of God, that ye present your bodies a living sacrifice, holy, acceptable unto God, which is

313

your reasonable service. And be not conformed to this world: but be ye transformed by the renewing of your mind, that ye may prove what is that good, and acceptable, and perfect, will of God." (Romans 12:1-2)

From this scripture I realize we are not here to be someone important as the world counts importance, but we are here to do the will of God. His will must always come before our own. God has a specific plan and purpose for each one of us, and unless we submit to Him and be transformed by renewing our mind through studying the Word, we will never reach the destiny God has planned for us. The Spirit must rule over the desires of the flesh. There is nothing on this earth that is more important than spending eternity with Jesus.

This is just a temporary period of time here on earth, while we work at the commission God has given us, to spread the good news to the world, and bring souls into the Kingdom of God. We are here as servants, not to be served.

Nothing we do in this world can add anything to what Jesus did for us on the cross. This was made very real to me one morning, as I was getting up; I was sitting on the side of the bed and thinking of what needed to be done that day, trying to get my priorities in order. Suddenly, from over my head and behind me, a very joyous voice came to me saying *"Rejoice because your name is written in the Lamb's Book of Life!"* I began to rejoice and thank God.

We get so caught up in our earthly agendas, that we forget that our plans are not nearly so important, compared to what Jesus did for us and for all eternity. We need to rejoice more often, because our names are written in the Lamb's Book of Life.

Our reservations are made! Hallelujah!

314

CONCLUSION

So, after 60 years, what has life taught me? He taught me that before we are born, God has a plan for our life. We are all born with certain talents and abilities that help make us who we are, and help us to become who He sees us to be. Sometimes those talents and abilities are never developed or they are buried, but with others they are developed through training, and are expanded to gain even greater abilities. When we are born again and are guided and directed by the Holy Spirit, He helps us develop our talents, and shows us how to use them to glorify God, and help others.

None of us realize the direction life is going to take us. We may have a plan, but God may have another plan. The devil definitely has a plan; his is to kill, steal, and destroy. God's plan for us is mentioned in Jeremiah 29:11 *"For I know the thoughts that I think toward you, says the Lord, thoughts of peace and not of evil, to give you a future and a hope."* He wants the very best for us. We get to choose who we will follow.

Many times, I've struggled with my plan, trying to make something happen. All I did was create a lot of anxiety and frustration within, and most of the time things did not turn out well or anything like I had hoped.

315

When I finally called out to God for help, He always showed me a "more perfect" way.

God has a destiny for each one of us. We all have a race to run. A person in a race prepares well, practices, trains, eats nutritiously, and does everything possible to be at their best. If we want to complete our race and finish the course that God has laid out for us, we need to do the same thing spiritually.

Paul spoke of this in the book of Hebrews.

"Wherefore seeing we also are compassed about with so great a cloud of witnesses, let us lay aside every weight, and the sin which doth so easily beset us, and let us run with patience the race that is set before us," (Hebrews 12:1-2)

We have to learn to hear God's voice, through His Word, through prayer, and just listening and meditating on His Word day and night. He will direct our path.

The storms of yesteryear and the miracles that brought me through those storms are the things that continue to help me get through the storms of today. When times get rough, I can remember the miracles, and know that God never changes, that He is alive and well, and still on the throne. He is working to complete the work He has begun in me, and will help me finish my race.

There are a lot of people that God brings into our life that help mold and make us who we are. As my friend, Betty Pope, once told me, it takes a diamond to cut another diamond; we all start out as diamonds in the rough. Rough diamonds have sharp edges that can hurt people, and God brings someone along to help smooth those edges. It may hurt at the time, but it's all part of the process of transforming us into His image.

I would say, the people that have helped with the greatest transformations of my life, have been my children: Bill, Kathy, Lynn, and Barbara, as well as my husband and extended family and friends. Each one is very distinctly different – no two are alike, jewels of great value, all with their own individual characteristics and talents. I would not be the person I am today without them. I've often wondered what kind of person I would have been, if I hadn't had them in my life, and of the priceless things I would have missed without them. Experiences and interaction with others are what mold our character. My children have been tremendously instrumental in helping to mold mine. I marvel at what God has done over 60 years, and it's still not over.

When I hear married couples say they "choose" not to have children, it makes my heart break. There is so much they will not learn. Our relationship with our children also helps us to understand our relationship with our heavenly Father. The scripture tells us that *"our children are a heritage of the Lord and the fruit of the womb is his reward."* (Psalm 127:3) The word heritage also means legacy, which means "achievement that continues after someone stops working, something that someone has achieved that continues to exist after they stop working or die." My children truly are my joy, my heritage and my legacy.

There were times in my life when I tried to change where I was going. I tried to change my vocation, and do something different, but every time I just couldn't make it happen. God knew where He was taking me, but I couldn't see it at the time.

When I look back over my life, I can see where every job I ever had taught me things that helped me with the job I have today. I thought I was there to earn a paycheck, when, in reality, I was in training for the things God had in store for me later.

When I became the director of Yavapai Food Bank, I began to realize these things. I discovered that God had brought me over a path to help me develop the skills I needed to get started, and He has continued to help me develop more as time goes on. He knows where he's taking me. I just needed to follow and be obedient.

So, I would say the greatest thing I have learned after 60 years can be summed up in two words – *TRUST HIM!*

FAVORITE SCRIPTURES

୬୬୬

Following is a short list of more of some of my favorite scriptures that I cherish and try to live by.

"Do not withhold good from those to whom it is due, when it is in the power of your hand to do so." (Proverbs 3:27 NKJV)

"He has shown you, O man, what is good; and what does the Lord require of you but to do justly, to love mercy, and to walk humbly with your God?" (Micah 6:8 NKJV)

"And whatever you do in word or deed, do all in the name of the Lord Jesus, giving thanks to God the Father through Him." (Colossians 3:17 NKJV)

"My little children, let us not love in word or in tongue, but in deed and in truth." (1 John 3:18 NKJV)

"For God so loved the world, that he gave his only begotten Son, that whosoever believeth in him should not perish, but have everlasting life. For God sent not his Son into the world to condemn the world; but that the world through him might be saved." (John 3:16-17 KJV)

"Therefore, whatever you want men to do to you, do also to them, for this is the Law and the Prophets." (Matthew 7:12-13 NKJV)

"And be ye kind one to another, tenderhearted, forgiving one another, even as God for Christ's sake hath forgiven you." (Ephesians 4:32 NKJV)

"But take heed to yourselves, lest your hearts be weighed down with carousing, drunkenness, and cares of this life, and that Day come on you unexpectedly. For it will come as a snare on all those who dwell on the face of the whole earth. Watch therefore, and pray always that you may be counted worthy to escape all these things that will come to pass, and to stand before the Son of Man." (Luke 21:34-36 NKJV)

"Now when these things begin to happen, look up and lift up your heads, because your redemption draws near." (Luke 21:28 NKJV)

"Let not your heart be troubled; you believe in God, believe also in Me. In My Father's house are many mansions; if it were not so, I would have told you. I go to prepare a place for you. And if I go and prepare a place for you, I will come again and receive you to Myself; that where I am, there you may be also. And where I go you know, and the way you know." Thomas said to Him, "Lord, we do not know where You are going, and how can we know the way?" Jesus said to him, "I am the way, the truth, and the life. No one comes to the Father except through Me." (John 14:1-6 NKJV)

MY MORNING PROCLAMMATION

ᑲᕽᑲᕽ

Proclamation based on the following scripture:
Psalm 118:24; Psalm 48:1; Romans 8:17,
2 Corinthians 5:7, Philipians 4:13, Psalm 18:2,
Acts 17:28, Psalm 32:7, Psalm 34:7, Psalm 119:165,
Psalm 112:1-3, 1 Peter 3:12, Ephesians 4:32,
Colossians 3:17, Psalm 103:1-5, Psalm 91:2.

"This is the day that the Lord hath made. I will rejoice and be glad in it. For great is my God and greatly is He to be praised. I am His child; I am an heir of God and joint heir with Jesus Christ. Therefore, no weapon that is formed against me shall prosper; for the weapons of my warfare are not carnal, but they are mighty through God to the pulling down of the enemy's strongholds. I am more than a conqueror; I am victorious because I walk by faith and not by sight and greater is He that is in me than he that is in the world. I can do all things through Christ who strengthens me, for The Lord is my rock, and my fortress, and my deliverer; my God, my strength, in whom I will trust; my buckler, and the horn of my salvation, and my high tower, For in him we live, and move, and have our being; ... we are his offspring. Thou art my

hiding place; thou shalt preserve me from trouble; thou shalt compass me about with songs of deliverance. The angel of the Lord encamps all around those who fear Him, and delivers them. Great peace have those who love Your law, and nothing causes them to stumble. Praise ye the Lord. Blessed is the man that feareth the Lord, that delighteth greatly in his commandments. His seed shall be mighty upon earth: the generation of the upright shall be blessed. Wealth and riches shall be in his house: and his righteousness endureth forever. For the eyes of the Lord are on the righteous, and His ears are open to their prayers; ...And be ye kind one to another, tender-hearted, forgiving one another, even as God in Christ Jesus forgave you. And whatsoever ye do in word or deed, do all in the name of the Lord Jesus, giving thanks to God and the Father by him. Bless the Lord, O my soul: and all that is within me, bless his holy name. Bless the Lord, O my soul, and forget not all his benefits: Who forgiveth all thine iniquities; who healeth all thy diseases; Who redeemeth thy life from destruction; who crowneth thee with lovingkindness and tender mercies; Who satisfieth thy mouth with good things; so that thy youth is renewed like the eagle's. I will say of the Lord, He is my refuge and my fortress: my God; in him will I trust.

More Family Photos

Lynn's son, Adam and his family currently live in Texas.

Adam & Liz Wedding - 1998

At right:
Family photo, 2008

Adam & Liz' children: Thomas, Valerie, and Crystal - 2011

Bill's three daughters:
Melissa 17, Amy 14,
Jenny 13 – 1993.

Currently they all live in
Longview, Washington

Melissa, Amy, Jenny – 2014

Bill's grandchildren L-R: Shaelyn, Haley, Kylie, Isaac, and Isaiah
Shaelyn, Isaac and Isaiah are Amy's children;
Haley and Kylie are Melissa's girls.

325

Bob's daughter Shari with her husband, Paul live in Buckeye, Arizona, and manage Hickman Farms.

Shari with her daughter, Jessica (several years ago)

Jessica currently is a wardrobe stylist and lives in New York 2013

Shari and Paul - 2008

Bob's daughter Robi with her husband, Dave, live in Iowa.
Their son Christopher, and granddaughter, Abigail live near by.

Below:
Chris and Robi.

Right:
Christopher's
daughter,
Abigail,
4 mos.

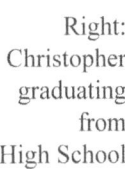

Christopher 13

Right:
Christopher
graduating
from
High School

327

Bob's son, Jim and wife Brenda, live in Pioneer Town, California; shown here with their three adopted grandchildren. L-R: Tyler 11, Isaiah 8, and Niki 7 - 2009.

Jim - 1998

At right are Jim and Brenda's children: Ryan, Nicole, Lori, and Dusty - 1984.

328

Above: Bella - 2013

Left: Lynn's daughter Angie, with her husband Rich, and Angie's adopted daughter Bella, live in Philadelphia.

Bottom: Angie and her daughter, Alix - 2013

Above: Alix with her daughter, Shanna, 2 wks. old. She lived in Philadelphia a few blocks from her mom, Angie, for several months but has since moved back to Texas.

Ann's younger brother, Dave with his wife, Kathy in 1990.
She has since passed away and Dave moved to the Prescott area
from Wisconsin, in late 2013.

Ann and Bob - 1994

Bob and Ann - 2008

Bob and Ann - 2011

Right: Ann and Bob
June 2014

Our new building is the metal building behind our original building at the left.. It is just under 5,000 sq. ft. and has a 20x20 freezer room and a 20x20 cooler room as well as the two we have in our original building. We had to begin using the freezer and cooler rooms before the building was signed off by the City of Prescott Valley. It was something needed for a very long time.

ADDENDUM

PART TWO

∽❧

AN ANSWER TO PRAYER FROM 2009

And all things, whatsoever ye shall ask in prayer,
believing, ye shall receive.
Ephesians 2:8-9 NKJV

One night, as I was driving to Life Christian University and praying and talking to God on the way; I was praying at the time for $24,000 to pay off our parking lot by the end of the year. When I said that prayer, the Lord spoke to my spirit, and said, "Is that all you want?"

I suddenly realized that I was limiting God. I said, "No, Lord, I want that food bank completely out of debt."

Later I added the need for another building as well.

That was in early 2009. The Lord told me to "Trust Him." The promise of the new building came in 2020 and was finished just before Christmas, when so much food is donated.

I'm not sure I could have held on to that promise for so many years, if He had not spoken those words to me. It was so very real that I could never forget it, and many times I would remind Him of His promise to me.

At the time I had made the first request of $24,000 to

pay off our parking lot, we were so destitute at the time that it was a struggle for me to even pay just $10 a month on the debt we owed.

After praying that prayer, about three months later, a special donation of $30,000 came in, which was very encouraging. We were able to pay off the parking lot. There was also the enormous request that our entire debts be paid off, which were both our new building on Long Mesa and the one on Spouse which at the time we had not been able to sell after moving from our Spouse location.

Meanwhile through the years, I continued to trust God concerning the payoff of our existing buildings. We finally were able to sell the building on Spouse in 2017, getting out from under one of the mortgages, and in 2020, we were were able to pay off the entire mortgage on our existing building on Long Mesa. PRAISE GOD!!!

After purchasing two smaller prefab buildings that were brought in and set up, we still desperately needed a larger building with additional freezer and cooler rooms to accommodate the growing needs of the food bank.

Time went by and we had gotten two or three prices to build a 3,000 sq. ft. building, and it seemed it would cost us at least $400,000 to $500,000 to add the needed space. This looked impossible, but I kept remembering God's promise and how He had told me to trust Him.

I kept trusting... and trusting... and trusting. I couldn't give up. I was sure I had heard right, so I kept on trusting.

Then in about 2017, we were surprised to receive a large legacy donation of $74,000.00. At that time, this was the largest one-time donations we had ever received. It was soon afterwards that we received another $50,000.00 legacy donation, and not long after that, another $72,000.00 legacy donation. These were very encouraging, but still not enough to get started on a new 3,000 square foot building.

We put an appeal letter out and sent them to all the foundations that we knew of and some local businesses. A little more came in, but still not enough to say we were ready to start building.

One of those letters had gotten to Mike Fann from Fann Contracting, and he came in one day, and said "I hear you need a new building." He looked everything over, saw how crowded we were, and said "We're not going to settle for a 3,000 sq. ft. building, we're going to put in a 5,000 sq. ft. building."

He talked like he was going to start in five minutes, and I said "We don't have enough money to get started on anything yet." He responded, "We're going to get the job done and you can pay me later."

One of our Board Trustees was very familiar with the person we needed to draw up the plans, so we thought we would at least get that part of the building started and could certainly pay for that, so we got started.

It was a little over two years going back and forth with our plans before we finally got them approved.

One night in church, our Pastor who knew of our need, prayed concerning the building and, in his prayer, I remember so well that he said "Lord, you're able to lay it on the hearts of the businesses in this area to donate to the food bank for this building until enough comes in."

That's just what happened. Over the two-year period that it took for the plans to be approved, enough came in from various sources so that we had enough to completely pay for the new building, as well as pay off the mortgage on our existing building.

No one can ever convince me that God does not answer prayer.

REFLECTION

It's very easy to get discouraged when our prayers are not answered immediately, but God is never late. He expects us to stand on His Word (the Bible) for the promises He makes. We have to believe first of all, that the Bible is the infallible Word of God.

Jesus said in John 15:7 "If ye abide in me, and my words abide in you, ye shall ask what ye will, and it shall be done unto you."

He wants to bless us, just as we want to bless our children. When they ask us for something they need, we give it to them, if we possibly can.

Another thing I learned through this experience, is that God is very generous. It's just as easy for him to answer something very little, as it is, to answer something very big; so don't be afraid to ask for "all" your needs.

When He asked me "Is that all you want," I became very aware of this principle. I was trying to be conservative, and only ask for what I considered to be an "emergency need."

My advice to all is that "don't be afraid to ask for the things that you need in this life. As long as you are walking and living according to His Word, He is willing to pour out many blessings in your life, if you can only 'Trust Him.'"

ADDINING, REMOVING AND CHANGING RESPONSIILITIES

ৡৡ

"Enlarge the place of your tent, stretch your tent curtains wide, do not hold back; lengthen your cords, strengthen your stakes. For you will spread out to the right and to the left; your descendants will dispossess nations and settle in their desolate cities.
Isaiah 54:2-3 NIV

One day in January, about 2014 or 2015, the Lord gave me this Word concerning my life. I felt He was telling me that I would be doing more in the next few months or years to come, than I had before.

By this time, I was still the Dean and, also an instructor at Life Christian University satellite campus in Prescott Valley. I was also a Chaplain at YRMC in Prescott Valley, which meant that one day, every two weeks, I would go to the hospital, visit each floor, praying for those in the hospital that wished to have prayer.

I loved that experience and felt that a lot more people were receptive to prayer than I had first imagined. After several months, I found it became harder and harder for me physically, to continue this job. It also took too much time away from the food bank. I finally just had to give it up. My legs were giving me more and more trouble.

I contacted Pastor Angie, our assistant Pastor at Living Faith Church, about teaching in the Women's Bible Study Class. Teaching has always been one of my first loves and I felt like it would be good to expand from just teaching at the University.

After teaching there for a while, one day Pastor Randy called me and asked if I would like to speak at the service for an upcoming Sunday night.

It was a little frightening at first, but I said "yes," I would give it a try. I remembered the scripture I had received from the Lord and wasn't sure if this was part of the answer or not.

I will never forget that night, I was so nervous that I wasn't sure I was going to be able to get through it.

Upon opening with prayer, the Lord knew how nervous I was, and suddenly I felt a special presence and anointing that was like a swishing sudden wind that came upon me from my feet up through the top of my head, and from then on I can hardly remember anything I said for the next 30-40 minutes.

I listened to the tape later, and it sounded like someone else. I couldn't believe it was me. I found myself listening intently to it, as though I was listening to someone for the first time.

Well, from that night, it has expanded over time to a full-time position of every Sunday night.

In August of 2014, I was ordained as an Associate Pastor of Living Faith Church and took on the responsibility of being the Financial Manager, which doesn't require much of my time. Meanwhile, I am still teaching at Life Christian University.

I also began teaching at one of the home group classes on Thursday nights, which was also very rewarding. This didn't last for too long though, because one day when getting out of my car at the foodbank, with my arms loaded down with "stuff," I tripped on a can that I hadn't seen and went down hard on my knees.

I landed so hard that I broke my left tibia bone just below the knee cap. That brought an end to all my teaching for a few weeks, and the home group never started up again.

That was the first serious broken bone I had, since I broke my ankle before when I was about 30 years younger. This was very different than my ankle situation. The pain was extremely more intense, and it took me a long time to be able to walk without a great deal of pain. Thankfully, our bodies heal eventually, and I was soon getting around as well as before.

REFLECTION

God made us who we are, and He knows us even better than we know ourselves. I have always been the type of person that unless I have so much to do that I am on the verge of collapsing, I am not happy.

After resigning my chaplain job, I was getting a little bored with so little to do, and God gave me more responsibilities. After several years though, as we get older and older, having a lot to do can become burdensome.

I was actually glad I had to let the home group teaching fall by the wayside. It had become a little too much to be going somewhere so many nights of the week.

I am always cautioning my daughter, Lynn, to be careful not to take on so much that it becomes over-burdensome. I can see that she is a lot like me, and I worry about all the responsibility that she takes on, but on the other hand, I did the same thing when I was her age.

I have come to the place where I accept the fact that everybody is different and there is more than one way to do things. My way is not the only right way. Others have a right to do things differently, and that is "finally" okay with me.

I have noticed that a lot of the character problems we have when we are young are gradually taken care of through old age. Finally, I am glad to get a nap every day when I get home from work and am not always looking for something more to do.

GOD SUSTAINS US ALL THE DAYS OF OUR LIFE

"Even to your old age and gray hairs I am he,
I am he who will sustain you.
I have made you and I will carry you;
I will sustain you and I will rescue you."
Isaiah 46:4 NIV

In June of 2016, Bob had to have a knee replacement, due to an accident while hunting. His knee was crushed and was beginning to bother him more and more. Finally, he agreed to see a doctor, who, after looking at the X-rays, wondered how he had even been able to walk.

Up until that time, he had a regular food pick up route at the Food Bank, which required him to lift at least 50 lbs. many times with every trip. He was still getting around pretty well, using knee braces, until finally the braces weren't working very well anymore.

Even though he was 83 at the time, he was in excellent health except for damage to his knee, so the doctor felt it would be fine for him to go ahead with the surgery.

He came through the surgery fine, and soon after

coming home, he started physical therapy. During that time, I took care of him, always had his medications and supplements ready for him each morning, cooked the meals, walked out to the mailbox every day for the mail and newspaper. We live on the back of nearly an acre and a half lot, so our driveway is very long which leads to the mailbox. I also took the trash barrel out to the road every week, and when walking back, sometimes I would have to stop and get my breath and rest a minute before continuing. I had five stents in my heart arteries so I thought they were good for life; however, from time to time, I noticed some pain in my chest, but a drink of water took care of it, and I never worried about it.

Bob got through with all his physical therapy and was starting to get around better and better. He finally took over more and more the things he had been doing before, and in a few months, everything was back to normal; however, Bob has never been quite as strong as he was before. The older you are, the harder it is to totally recover from a major health issue.

One morning when I got up, I was having a tremendous back ache mostly in my upper back, and feeling very weak. I was trying to get breakfast ready, and I finally felt like I was going to pass out. I didn't want to fall, so I made it to the kitchen table just in time, and laid my head down on the table. I began to feel sick like I wanted to throw up, but hadn't eaten anything yet.

Bob came in, and I told him I was feeling strange and thought I was going to be sick, and he rushed the trash basket over to me. By that time, my chest pains began to increase, and he called 911. They barely had gotten there, when suddenly I didn't remember anything else. They said I had passed out. I regained consciousness on a hard cold surface and opened my eyes to a woman over me doing something. I said, "Where am I?" and she said "You're on the floor. We're getting you ready to go to the hospital."

I had a heart attack and passed out. In the ambulance, I got sick again, and they provided a bag for me, then the medic gave me a cherry flavored aspirin and told me to chew it up quickly. I soon was feeling better and by the time I got to the hospital I felt good enough to go home, but they wanted to do a stress test, so I had to stay until the next day when I could take a stress test. The nurse came in later in the evening and said they cancelled the stress test for the next morning, because my heart was still under a great amount of stress, and if I left the hospital and did any exertion, it would probably cause a more severe heart attack.

I was in the Prescott Valley Hospital for about four days, while they were trying to decide what to do.

Finally, they came in and said they were moving me to the Prescott Hospital, where they were better able to care for Cardiac patients.

At the Prescott Hospital I was there an additional eight days, while they cleaned out as much plaque in the old stents as possible, and then recommended a bypass operation. I began to pray for God's intervention, because I thought, at that time, it sounded like that was what they intended to do, and the only thing that would help.

Later, one of the doctors came in and told me she felt I was too "frail" to go through a bypass. I was glad she recommended not to have it, but I didn't like the word "frail." I had never been "frail" in my life, and I didn't like the sound of it.

Another doctor came in and said he had recommended that they do more stents inside the existing stents, because I wasn't a good candidate for bypass surgery.

Dr. Assar was the doctor that did the procedures,

which took over an hour on just the first artery. He tackled it first, and according to him "it really kicked his butt!" The artery was not a straight shot and wound around crazily. He had to really take his time to get through it, but it was very successful.

Then two days later he did the rest of the stents in less than an hour. When finished, he said "You are as good as though you had a bypass." You should be okay for several years." I really liked this doctor.

God has been very good to me to give me such great medical care and terrific doctors through the years.

Since that time, my body has gotten weaker, and harder for me to go places, and do things, like I did before.

I feel I'm just about "spent" here in this world, and my parting time may be pretty close. I hope I don't sound shocking, but I am looking forward to going to heaven, seeing Jesus, and receiving a new, youthful body, and living forever in a glorious environment. This world is getting more difficult for me every day.

REFLECTION

Recently I was reflecting on the past year and realized how God had protected me during the time of Bob's recovery and I was sustained until he was completely recovered and strong enough again to help care for me.

If I had a heart attack while he was still recovering and unable to walk very well, it would have been hard on both of us. Even little things like this are a great blessing.

I have come to realize that God is not finished with me yet. Until He calls me home, I will be faithful to do the things He has for me to do.

Bob (89) and Ann (86), in the middle, at the City Council meeting where Bob received a plaque for recognition of 29 years of service as a Volunteer with the Prescott Valley Police Department. At the left is Jeremy Martin, the acting Chief of Police in Prescott Valley. On the right side is the Prescott Valley City Mayer, Kell Palguda.

Above are most of our children, grand children, great grand-children, and great, great grandchildren, and some great, great, great grandchildren. Some photos were not available.

FINAL WORDS

୭ଏ

To our childrren, grandchildren and to their children,
and to their children, and to all those yet to come.

Hearken unto me now therefore, O ye children,
and attend to the words of my mouth. Let not thine heart
decline to her ways, go not astray in her paths.
Prov 7:24-25 KJV

Misfortune pursues the sinner, but prosperity is the
reward of the righteous. A good man leaves an
inheritance for his children's children, but a sinner's
wealth is stored up for the righteous.
Proverbs 13:21-22 NIV

An inheritance for our children and our children's
children is not always money or other natural things of
this world, but the greatest legacy of all is a good name,
of those who trusted in their God, and lived righteously
in a very controversial world.

Every morning our prayers from your father and
myself are that all our children, our grandchildren, our
great grandchildren, and all that are to come, will find

347

God, if they don't already know Him, that the blood of Jesus and His grace and mercy will cover them and will forgive all their sins, never to be remembered anymore. It doesn't matter how big or little we think our sins are, we are all born in sin, inherited from the first humans of God's new creations, Adam and Eve.

Because mankind inherited the sin nature, their destiny was to perish and be cast into the Lake of Fire when they died. The soul of man never dies. This is the inner man that will live forever "somewhere!"

Before the foundation of the world, God knew beforehand what was going to happen, so he provided a way of escape for all of mankind to be saved from that terrible punishment that was prepared only for Satan, the fallen angels, and all his demons. He sent his only begotten son, Jesus, to become a human sacrifice for our sins. In the Old Testament, they had to take an animal and sacrifice it once a year, and even more often if they sinned in between, and the blood from that animal was laid on the mercy seat for atonement for their sins, but Jesus fulfilled the law and no longer do they have to have an animal sacrifice every year. Jesus became our sacrifice by shedding his own blood for our sins, once and for all. He fulfilled The Old Testament laws when he did this. It took His blood to pay the ransom for our freedom from Satan's kingdom and provided a way to transfer us into the Kingdom of God. He delivered us from death and the destruction of our souls, and He also paid the price for our good health and the healing of our body when he was beaten terribly by the Roman soldiers at Pilot's command. He was so severely beaten that his back was slashed to ribbons down to the bone. This was so we could be healed and never have to suffer such pain.

The crown of thorns that they pressed down on his head were sharp and some say they were up to 3 to 4 inches long. This was also part of the blood shed for us, and the remainder flowed out of His side when a soldiers stuck his spear in to make sure he was dead.

He suffered great pain when He took our sins upon Himself on the cross. It is said in scripture that his body became distorted, twisted, until he didn't even look like a man. That is what sin can do. This is part of the great suffering he bore for the healing of our bodies and the redemption of our souls.

On the third day, He rose again from the dead and won victory over Satan, death, hell, and the grave. Because of that victory, we too have the same victory and will also be raised again from the dead when the Trumpet of God sounds. At that time all believers in the grave will rise, no longer with corruptible bodies, but with incorruptible, immortal bodies to live forever and ever. Most people call this the "rapture of the Church," or as some call it "the catching away," which all true believers are part of.

When we do sin and feel conviction and repent of it, we just have to say a quick prayer and ask forgiveness of our sins, and he removes them completely and erases it from our lives forever. It is also erased from our Book that is kept in heaven. Jesus is the only way to the Father God, and to receive everlasting life for all eternity. He said in:

John 14:6 *"...I am the way, the truth, and the life: no man cometh unto the Father, but by me.*

There is no other way. There will be many decivers that will rise up in the last days that will say there is more than one way to heaven, but it isn't true. The only way to ensure that you are not deceived is to get better acquainted with your Bible. Read it daily, for in it you have hope of eternal life.

After we are ransomed from out of Satan's kingdom, we are transferred into the Kingdom of God. We are also adopted into the family of God, as his children. We now have His Name and are "heirs of God and joint heirs with Jesus Christ." We now have the righteousness of God within us, and the Holy Spirit (the third person of the Godhead) within us to lead and guide us into all truth.

His mercy and grace will follow us now all the days of our life, and we will dwell in the house of the Lord forever. He gives you hope and a future in this life.

Jer. 29:11 (NIV) *For I know the plans I have for you," declares the Lord, "plans to prosper you and not to harm you, plans to give you hope and a future.*

We know where our final resting place will be, in heaven itself, and alive forevermore; no more death, no more sorrow, no more pain or suffering, with lots to do, including fun things. Your days will be filled with plenty. The earth is a shadow of Heaven. The things we like here on earth may be in heaven in some form. God knows what we like even better than we do. He will make sure we enjoy our life in heaven.

Here on earth Jesus was the King of the Jews and He always will be, but He is also King and Ruler over all the powers and rulers on the earth even now. He also raises up Kings and Rulers and can just as quickly put them down when they rebel against Him and His plans.

There will eventually be a new earth. The old one we have now will totally burn up and pass away, but God will make all things new, and there is where we will rule and reign forever with Him.

Because we are now part or the Royal Family, we are also going to be Kings and Priests on the earth in the world to come. We are going to rule and reign with Him throughout eternity. The Bible says we will judge angels. Heaven is a busy place, and lots to do. I won't take time to try to name everything that I know about, or things that I have heard of from others that have been there, but I can guarantee it will not be boring. You also will be young again with a glorified, immortal body, and strength that you didn't know you could ever have, so nothing will be tedious or difficult. You can do anything you want in heaven, and nothing can hurt you. You can jump off a cliff and just be suspended in air, or gradually go to the bottom, just by your thoughts. There is no gravity there. You will not need to take up time sleeping and cooking (unless you want to). You will have a beautiful mansion made uniquely just for you, decorated just the way you like. He knows you better than you know yourself. Heaven is a very mammoth, large place that keeps expanding with everyone that goes there, including things that make them happy. There is a great deal of fun and entertainment to enjoy as well, and the angels many times enjoy them with you.

We also pray that none of our children will just carry Jesus' name in their pocket, but will put Him in their heart, that they will come to know him personally, knowing that He always hears their prayers, is with them always, helps them in their troubles, restores their soul, and prepares a righteous path for them to walk on.

We also pray that God would bless the work of their hands that they would be prosperous in all that they do, increase their substance in the land, and that wealth and riches be in their house always, and they would be kind and generous in all of their ways, helping others and always walk in love and unity with each other and others in the body of Christ. That they would always esteem others as highly as they do themselves.

We especially pray that you would all find your place

in the earth as the Holy Spirit guides you, where you're supposed to live, and what you're supposed to do, and that all of you would come to the place of fulfilling your destiny and purpose that God has ordained for each of you and for all of the people on earth, from before the foundation of the world.

You are not here on the earth at this particular time by chance. You were destined to be here at this time from before the foundations of the earth. Even our purposes have been ordained ahead of time for us.

Acts 17:26 *From one man he made every nation of men, that they should inhabit the whole earth; and he determined the times set for them and the exact places where they should live.–* (NIV)

We also pray that you all would live long lives, walking uprightly before God and helping others in life along the way. This is how we eventually find our purpose. If we follow God's Word and try to live according to His will, He will lead us into it. We don't know ahead of time what our purpose is or the time of our departure from the earth.

Yet, some people will not die at all. Those are the ones of the cherished Bride of our Lord Jesus that will be caught away in the rapture and taken to heaven without tasting of death. They will be changed from the mortals that they are in this world, to immortal ones, to live forever and forever. I mentioned this in more detail above.

Those that are lukewarm and distant from the Lord, even though they may call themselves by the name of "Christian," will be left behind to experience the terrible years of tribulation on the earth. The anti-Christ will be in charge at that time, and those that profess to be Christians and will not deny their faith, nor obey the anti-Christ by taking the "mark of the beast," will be killed either outright, probably through beheading, or by starving to death. No one will be able to buy food or anything else without the mark of the beast. Those that take the mark of the beast will be doomed for all eternity. Parents will have to make a choice to either see their children starve to death or take the mark. (These, of course, are children born after the rapture.) It will be a terrible time to live and right choices will be very hard or nearly impossible to make.

Jesus says plainly that anyone that denies Him, He (Jesus) will also deny before His heavenly father.

Matt 10:33 (KJV) *But whosoever shall deny me before men, him will I also deny before my Father which is in heaven.*

To be ready for the rapture when Jesus returns is so very important. Keep your lamps lit with the Holy Spirit of God in you. Do not get carried away by the temptations of the world, and we will see you all in heaven one day.

Remember, everything in this world is just temporary, but heaven is forever (and so also is the lake of fire). Nothing in this world should be so important for us that we would lose our soul over.

THE END

Back Cover:

Miracles in the Midst of Storms leads us on a personal journey in the life of a woman of faith, the miracles she witnesses, and her absolute reliance on God which sustains her through her storms.

Ann Wilson, author and main character of this memoir, humbly invites us to immerse ourselves in the pages of this biographical journey. Wisdom, honesty, humor, transparency, and relevance all play their part in molding the paragraphs to tangible, relatable conversations filled with joy, trials, pain, faith, and an ultimate surrendering to the Will of God. Ann's wisdom and humility are a continuous thread throughout the book, and quietly encased in her words, "I realize that every answer to prayer is a miracle."

Scriptural quotes adds both substance and grace to her lessons learned, which gently encourages us to ponder our own lives, thereby guiding us to recognize our own miracles that are veiled behind our storms. Faith and perseverance then navigates us to a safe place, where gates open to discover that the miracles have always been there, waiting patiently to be lifted from the outstretched hands of God.

Ann and her husband Bob moved to their residence in Dewey, Arizona, in June 1992, where they lived the remainder of their days. Ann was the Dean and Instructor of Life Christian University – Prescott Valley campus for eight years, Volunteer and Director of Yavapai Food Bank with her husband, Bob, for 30 years, an ordained Associate Pastor of Living Faith Church, Chaplain, teacher, mother, and a faithful child of Almighty God.

—Russell Womack
(revised slightly to update)